THE DESERT IS
MY OASIS

THE DESERT IS MY OASIS

Poems

HISHAM ALI HAFIZ

Foreword by Peter Mansfield

KEGAN PAUL INTERNATIONAL
London and New York

First published in 1994 by
Kegan Paul International Ltd
PO Box 256, London WC1B 3SW, England

Distributed by
John Wiley & Sons Ltd
Southern Cross Trading Estate
1 Oldlands Way, Bognor Regis
West Sussex, PO22 9SA, England

Columbia University Press
562 West 113th Street
New York, NY 10025, U.S.A.

© Hisham Ali Hafiz 1994

Phototypeset in 10 on 12pt Palatino, by Intype, London

Printed in Great Britain by TJ Press, Padstow, Cornwall

ISBN 0 7103 0483 8

British Library Cataloguing in Publication Data

Hafiz, Hisham Ali
  Desert is My Oasis: Poems
  I. Title
  892

  ISBN 0–7103–0483–8

US Library of Congress Cataloging in Publication Data

Hafiz, Hisham Ali, 1931–
  The desert is my oasis : poems / Hisham Ali Hafiz.
    p. cm.
  Translated from Arabic.
  Includes index.
  ISBN 0–7103–0483–8 : $76.50
  I. Title.
  PJ7828.F49D48 1994   94-6554
  892'.716—dc20   CIP

CONTENTS

FOREWORD

By Peter Mansfield

By any standards this book is a publishing event of considerable interest. Because the Saudi Arabian author is the publisher of the largest group of newspapers and magazines in the Arab World, the equivalent for the anglophone reader would be to find that one of our media magnates – say Mr Rupert Murdoch or Viscount Rothermere – had recorded their innermost thoughts and feelings about mankind and the world in incandescent words of poetry. It is the more extraordinary that these compositions come from the heart of the Arabian Peninsula. This is where Arabic poetry as well as the Islamic religion were born, but for many centuries the mainsprings of Arab/Muslim literary creativity moved westwards and northwards to the Levant, Iraq, North Africa and Anadalusia. Now the Peninsula is showing signs of a literary renaissance and one of the pleasures of these poems is that they so obviously derive from the Arabian Desert which Hisham Ali Hafiz calls his oasis.

They are personal and idiosyncratic – owing little to any literary tradition. Hafiz may have been educated in Egypt but his Arabian roots are unimpaired. He prefers not to think of these writings as poems. *Kalimat laha Iqa'* or 'Words with Rhythm' was his chosen title in Arabic; 'I am a messenger from prose to poetry,' he says on p.75. It is true that since the 1940s there has been a strong tradition of 'free verse' in Arabic which broke from the long-standing classical heritage and is usually thought to have begun with the Iraqi poets Nazik al-Malaikah and Badr Shakir al-Sayyab. But Hafiz clearly feels that he does not belong to their school. Yet western readers will have no hesitation in identifying these compositions as poetry.

The poems are at the same time highly personal and universal. The poet speaks of his family ties, his objects of love and admiration and his relationships with his own society. He reacts, at times with fierce pride, to what his fellows say about him and his poetry.

But he is also concerned with wider issues such as the loss of Palestine, the relationship between Arabism and Islam and above all the attitudes of his fellow-Muslims and himself to God and the Prophet. In fact the poems are intensely religious in feeling – even when they are apparently dealing with secular matters such as the balance between erotic and platonic love as in the fine poem 'We Leave Something for Love' (p.71).

At times the tone is pensive and mystical ('My Soul Found Comfort in the Presence of God', p.109) but there are also great outbursts of rage ('Poison is an Old Weapon of Treachery', p.13). However, the poet convinces the reader that it is possible to be passionate in your faith without becoming a scowling fanatic. He is an enemy of such people and excoriates them with splendid scorn:

> Their books are upside-down;
> Their thoughts are impaired;
> Their views are defective,
> They curse beauty and grace
> They throw themselves into the bosom of barren valleys,
> Swim in morbid seas,
> Drink from poisoned rivers,
> Welcome extremism and the harrassment of others,
> And betray innocent Muslims.

The translation of poetry is not for the faint-hearted; some would say it is impossible and should never be tried. The combination in one individual of a linguistic scholar and a poet, such as Arthur Waley the great translator of Chinese poetry, is rare indeed. Sometimes the collaboration of two such men as the Egyptian Ibrahim Shukrullah and the English poet John Heath-Stubbs in their translations of Arabic poetry can achieve fine results. But again this seldom happens.

It would be a mistake to assume that translation of Arabic prose-poetry such as this is relatively easy because it lacks rhyme or metre. How do you turn 'words with rhythm' in another tongue? Arabic verbal rhythm is esoteric because it derives from the structure of the language based on the triliteral root. This means that hundreds of words derived from different roots have similar forms and therefore identical rhythms because the three root letters are inflected or prefixed in the same way, to express particular variations, in the use as nouns or verbs, of the basic concept that these three letters represent. (Thus *d-r-s* signifies study and *madrassa* a school; *k-t-b* indicates writing and *maktaba* a library.) Hence the great Arabic tradition of *saj'* or 'rhyming prose'. It is the architecture of Arabic that matters. The nineteenth-century German philosopher, von Schelling, said, 'Architecture in general is frozen music'; one might say that a line of Arabic poetry is a row of harmonious buildings that have been melted into melody.

In the face of these difficuties it is hard to see how this translation could have been improved. Without sacrifice of meaning the lines have their rhythm although inevitably it is of a different kind from the Arabic. The result provides a rare insight into the thoughts and feelings of an unusual individual in a distant land. For any westerner who is not smugly content with his own culture it offers an attractive opportunity to enjoy a stimulating and unusual glimpse of a part of the eastern world.

London,
April 1994

PART ONE

Supplications and Entreaties

I Pray to the Immortal, the Everlasting

In this year,
In all years,
In days that are past
And days to follow,
I pray to God to intensify my belief
And to strengthen my mind and faith.

I pray to the Immortal, the Everlasting,
The Almighty Lord,
The Source of Peace,
The Guardian of Faith, the Dominant,
The Originator, the Glorious,
The Exalted, the Irresistible, the Supreme,
The Creator, the Evolver, the Bestower of Forms,
To Him belong the Most Gracious Names,
Whatever is in the Heavens and on Earth,
Such as air, water,
Shades, inanimate objects, and creatures,
Sings His Praises and Glorifies Him.

I make the same requests and pray for the same things,
Make the same wishes and entertain the same hopes,
Appealing to Him Who changes or stabilizes the hearts of men,
To Him Who is tender, Bestower of honour and of great favours,
To protect me from the severity of the humiliation of slips,
The severity of the slips of those who walk in the shade of death,
To stabilize my heart with firm belief
And with a conviction in the truth of the Appointed Time
And of the Day on which disbelievers,
Traitors, hypocrites, and atheists are penalized.
My Lord, my God,
Grant me my wishes, and accept my prayers,
My Lord, my God,
Accept the excuse of a repentant servant,
Who has great hopes in Your Mercy,

Looks forward to Your Forgiveness,
Kneels down for Your Grace,
And prostrates himself before Your Majesty,
With the passion of a runaway, full of hope,
Weeping because of the sins he has committed,
Running away from Hell,
Hoping for Paradise and the Light,
Keen to secure Your Mercy,
Immersed in Your Bounty,
And submerged in Your Benevolence.

There is no God but You,
The Immortal, Self-Subsisting, Eternal One,
You have no partner,
There is no one near to You in majesty,
I send blessings to Your Prophet,
And I salute the one You favour,
There is no God but You,
You have no partner.

No, God has no In-Laws

No, God has no in-laws
God is the One and Only, the Absolute.
No dictator has ever happened
To rule this country
But has managed to find
Some hypocrite who sings for him, chanting,
Before all creatures, all the people,
'I am an enemy of God's,'
Should the oppressor ask him to do so,
Should the dictator order him to chant such notes.
He impudently and shamelessly would declare,
'This is the best of all countries,'
While wickedly whispering in private,
'This is the worst of all countries.'

One day in our time, we have seen,
As we seen in former days
And is seen in every period,
A cunning person and a deluded one.
The cunning person cajoles, flatters and argues pertinaciously.
He masquerades as a patriot and a poet.
He says to heavy boots and to whips,
'I shall sell the mob a train,
The train of atheism and socialism,
And I shall buy you, from intellectuals,
All paper and pens, as well as freedom.
I shall draw the rug and the carpet
From underneath the faith of Islam.'
He competes with his own mirror reflection
And thinks that an exit
From the rot of prostitutes
Could be made by a hypocricy
In dealing with tyranny, with blind power.
You are well-known for your impudence!
You live in violated sanctities!

You have used your verse to clap
For the first setback in our world!
You are the one who has said to the first inflated cat
On our soil, on our remains,
'You are Grace, incarnated; you are the leader.'

Your secret has been exposed,
So arrangement of words,
Verse propaganda,
Defence,
Hiding behind a mask,
Pretending to be on the side of
The oppressed and subdued –
None of these can redeem your sins,
Nor dilute your atrocities and offences.
We have monitored what you say.
You say,
With the lines, between the lines,
Above the lines, under the lines,
In a word or with a poem, or with an expression,
Addressing the master who stands on a tank,
'My Lord! If you hear
Some clamour or some clowning
Or if some agitation and commotion
Reach your ears, my Lord,
Or if hands collide, my Lord,
Clapping noisily,
Rest assured, my Lord,
As this is the art of giving a sense of relief
To souls and spirits,
If, my Lord,
I describe Abu Bakr, the Honest, as a liar;
Umar, the Arbitor, as an unjust person;
And Khalid Ibn Al-Walid as a coward –
If I speak of the Caliphate in Andalusia,
The leadership in Damascus,
The learning in Baghdad,
And the light in Makkah, Medina and Al Quds,
As mere falsehoods and trivialities
I am only opening for you, my Lord,
The doors to a time-honoured glory.'

6

'With great modesty,
I, my Lord, and You
Are in the same boat.
And I do not want your armament
To be defeated,
Nor my poetry
To be wiped out,
After all, as you know, my Lord,
As you are fully aware, my Lord,
I am your hired servant;
I do not want oppression
To lead to an explosion
In the camps and castles of my Lord.'

'I have a prescription, for my Lord,
That is not like smallpox or measles,
And yet it kills, eliminates, and annihilates,
Much more than cholera or the plague can do.
It is like injustice and inequity
Like torture and repression,
Or to use current idioms,
It is like AIDS and cancer.
Listen to me, my Lord,
Let me manoeuvre and strike
At stable societies and countries;
Let me arrange a wedding for your fires;
Let me bury in the folds of my poetry
The skeletons and skulls of victims.
Let me make drugged listeners feel that
The masses listen
Only to your programme,
Your Listeners' Choice,
Or rather, Hypocrites' Forgeries.

Listeners' Choice,
Or Hypocrites' Forgeries, my Lord,
Is the medicine and the treatment.
For, whenever I attack the symbols,
Pretend to have an encounter with humiliation,
Perform prayers in the Garden of Evil,
Make fun of Holidays and Fridays

And mock the caliphs, the righteous, the angels,
And the Creator Himself –
I am only forcing listeners to be
Dazzled and amazed,
To make them forget to think and reflect,
And drag them behind me,
Fully occupied with controversies and quarrels,
So that the field,
The area that is left,
May be clear, for my Lord,
Do you see, my Lord,
What an obedient servant I am?
How submissive to you and how humble I am?
How I admire your recklessness
And am enthralled with your violence?
How greatly I hope
To live in your shade,
Kissing the fake medals on your chest,
Praying to the belt around the waist,
And enjoying the warmth of your dagger.

We say to you,
'No, there are not, and there will never be,
No relatives or in-laws for God.
God is the One and Only, the Absolute.
No ruler has ever happened
To rule this country
But has managed to find
Some hypocrite like you who beats the drums or plays the pipe
Before all creatures, before all people
And says to the crowds,
'I am an enemy of God's.'
But those who have read history know,
And those who live will see
What will happen,
What has frequently happened,
To God's enemies.

But What is There in the Unseen?

I am eighty years old.
This means, I am,
Age-wise,
On a road, the road of years,
Of which I don't know when
The end will come,
When the hours, the minutes, the seconds of my life would stop.
I do not know whether the days will restore
The youth that has gone by,
Has passed away,
or, if you will,
What time has done to my destiny.

First and last,
I thank this Powerful, the Almighty,
That I, in this old age,
Can sleep
In any excited evening,
And I can harness my unruly desires
And my unfair heart.

But what is there in the Unseen?
And what is there in the heart of the silence?
And what is there in the perplexed mind?

Have I been wretched?
Have I grudged every achievement?
Have I been ambitious one?
Have I envied every success?
Have I been happy?
Have I enjoyed happy occasions?
Have I seen both good and bad times?
Definitely, I have seen both,
Just as all creatures,
And all mankind, have.

But, what do I wish for,
Having reached the age of eighty?
I wish for truthfulness.
I wish for being freed.
I wish for love, for adoration,
Of the Lord of the universe and of humanity.
I wish, as a faithful worshipper does,
For His mercy, His pardon,
In this age,
In these last days of mine.

My Mother Turned her Eyes to the Creator and Wept

I have reconciled myself to blackness!
I have forced myself to utter
Expressions that yearn for separation.
I have tamed my heart to submit
To oppression, remoteness, and insomnia.
Excuse me! Pardon me!
Blackness within me leads and dominates.

I have taken wounds for my ally,
Pus for my mate.
My grudge has discovered a friend.
My vengeance is my companion.
Excuse me! Pardon me!
Blackness within me leads and dominates.

I have quarrelled with happiness.
I have forgotten my Lord and His worship.
I have learned to be obscene.
I have trained myself to be insolent.
My night knows no sleep.
My morning no waking up.
Excuse me! Pardon me!
Blackness within me leads and dominates.

I have been a student of debauchery.
I have become a professor of lechery.
I have started a great school
For degradation and loss, and for villains.
My fortune is bad luck.
My emblem is black cat.
That plays and has fun in ruins.
Excuse me! Pardon me!
Blackness within me leads and dominates.

On a green and white day,
On the night I was wed to repentance,
A night of the month of light,
My mother turned her eyes to the Creator and wept
On the Night of Qadr, in the Month of Bounty.
My mother begged the Almighty, and she prayed
That my Lord may guide my course,
May forgive me,
May pardon my sins;
That I may fast, pray, and worship God,
May become an embodiment of the Fear of God,
May become an example to be followed.
The Most Gracious, Most Kind the One who is ready to answer
Granted my mother what she prayed for.
I am thankful and grateful to God first,
And then to my mother.

Poison is an Old Weapon of Treachery

In this brownish grey age, some people have appeared
Who are like beasts, like cracks, like the stone,
Like a sphinx, like oppression, like a crow,
Like tombs, like mirage, like torture –
People who change the most simple into most difficult,
Transform what is good into a wide-spreading evil,
Turn self-esteem, and sense of honour and pride
Into prevalent humiliation,
And replace green paradise
With a blazing hell.

Their books are upside-down;
Their thoughts are impaired;
Their views are defective.
They curse beauty and grace
Throw themselves into the bosom of barren valleys,
Swim in morbid seas,
Drink from poisoned rivers,
Welcome extremism and the harassment of others,
And betray innocent Muslims.

They wear gloomy clothes,
Uphold red slogans,
And put on their lips
Barren, yellowish smiles.
Their souls are vindictive and foreboding,
With slow death oozing out.
They wear on their faces
A grumbling, cruel frown.
They glare with bold eyes,
Which know no shame and never forget a thing.
They put on square faces,
Which are never embarrassed, never have mercy.
Their ears are closed and deaf.
Their mouths are tight and never smile.

They say, or actually they claim,
'We are advanced, and you are backward.'
They say, or actually they claim,
'We are happy, and you are miserable.'
They say, or actually they claim,
'We are well guided and you are at a loss.'
They say, or actually they claim,
'You are at the very bottom,
We are at the top.'

May God guide you and pardon you;
Ugliness is one of Satan's features,
Treachery is one of the devil's recommendations,
And extremism is a sign of madness.
A Muslim is a well-balanced person.
God is Light and Beauty.
Muhammad is a Lamp, shining and shedding light.
Gloominess and fear
Are calamities and signs of uncertainty.
Frowning is a sign of haughtiness and arrogance.
The truth, told with an intention to deceive,
Is the currency of hypocrites.
Injustice, cruelty, and double crossing
Are some of the traits of tyrant unbelievers.
Poison is an old weapon of treachery.
Misery is a breeze coming from hell.
Modesty is the shield of Muslims.
God, the Beautiful, the Most Gracious, the Most Merciful,
Loves beauty and loves the compassionate.

I pray for you and on your behalf,
I entreat God, with all His Majesty and Glory.
Yes I pray to Him, Who will admit
Into His paradise
Those who believe and who say,
'There is no God but God,
And Muhammad is the Prophet of God.'

I pray and ask forgiveness, and I hope
We will all swim together
In the sea of repentance,

We will be cleansed and drink our fill from
The spring of God's forgiveness,
And we will all be
Rightly guided.

As a Palestinian who Trusted and Believed

If Time frowns,
I appeal for relief from You.
If there seems to be nowhere to go,
I seek refuge with You.
And when I get lost on my way,
I run back to walk in Your path.
When all springs dry up,
I quench my thirst out of the purity of Your Mercy,
O my Lord, O my God!

How misled and how misleading am I!
How I crave for the bitter taste of things that are forbidden,
Plant the spearhead
In the heart of what is legitimate,
I wake up with my eyes fixed,
With a host of illusions
Colliding against me and shaking me.
I return looking for outlets
From my affliction, wretchedness, and misery,
And from my sins.
I do find no way out
Other than by the Glory of Your Face,
The greatness of Your Pardon,
The generosity of Your Forgiveness, and
The clemency of Your Power,
O my Lord, O my God!

Whenever loved ones get cool with me,
Whenever friends keep at a distance from me,
Whenever a friend finds
A friend other than me – I find myself all alone,
Like a particle of sand in the desert,
Or a shrub in a wasted garden –

Like a Palestinian who trusted and believed
His most bitter enemy,
And thereby lost his tears
And his hopes,
And chains and feelings of hatred
Flourished in the land of his afflictions;
Nothing was left for him, except to keep saying,
'O my Lord! O my God!'

Days Consume my Life

Yesterday and today for me are the same.
My day starts with work,
While yesterday ended
With the hope and expectation
That the following day
Would be better than the current and the past.
My life is being consumed by days.

My future and my tomorrow?
What about my future and my tomorrow?
Am I one of the happy lot?
Or of the miserable?
I am lost in anticipation?
Days consume my life!

I waste hours in misery
And spend others in happiness.
Many hours die of boredom,
Others are spent awake because of insomnia.
Many hours are on fire from restlessness,
Others are lost in weariness.
Many hours are fed on blame,
Others are hungry for some sleep.
Many hours are waiting for other hours
To prove they exist and are alive
Days consume my life.

The days of waiting
For brief moments of happiness
Blow up, like cyclones,
My sweetest times
And my most beautiful hours.
They bring me back, wounded and in chains,
To the nights of fear.
What does my destiny have in store for me?

What will happen to my parents and relatives?
What will happen to my children and my wife?
What have I built and made?
Days consume my life.

I never cease to travel, going and coming back,
Boarding aircraft, vehicles, and ships.
In the richest countries, there is much that I enjoy,
And in the poorest I share the pain of afflicted people.
I see God's worshippers enslaving
God's creatures,
And I witness God's worshippers worshipping
God's creatures.
I am amazed to see
Scholars, both strong and rich,
Who do not believe in God
Nor appreciate His blessings.
I get surprised to see savage beasts
Afraid of a weak human being.
I get shocked to see a muscular person
Made captive of alcohol
Or being wasted by drugs.
Days consume my life!

Woe to me from women,
What a beautiful one can do to me!
She only has to wink at me and I am lured,
While her heart is beating for others.
So I boil up, explode, and burst,
Shouting, storming, turning everything upside down.
I spend years and years
In war and hard toil,
In fits and starts,
In manoeuvres, skirmishes, and truce.
Days consume my life.

I wake up with a headache,
Colic in the stomach,
And pain in the joints;
My ears hear nothing,
My eyesight is poor,

My body shakes,
And my face is wrinkled.
I fail to perform
The act of love.
My rancour, deeply rooted in my heart,
Blocks the way
To reconciliation and peace,
And to forgiveness and forgetting.
Days consume my life.

I wake up to the voice of the prayer-caller;
He repeats again and again,
'Come to prayer;
Come to success.'
Then I renounce the world,
And shiver in fear of the Hereafter;
I perform my prayers, fast and perform Haj;
I circumambulate the Ancient House
And walk between Safa and Marwa,
Just as my grandmother, Hajir, did.
I visit my beloved one, Muhammad the Trustworthy;
I ask God's blessings for him and salute him
And his two Companions.
And in the grave-yard at Al-Beqi',
I pray and ask for mercy, particularly for
My father, brother, grandfather and uncle,
And all my dead relatives and the relatives of God's Prophet,
And his Companions.
In secret, I curse
The unfaithful, the malevolent and the unbeliever.
Days consume my life.

Whether I am here or there,
Wherever I am,
Whatever the time is,
I wait for me end,
Hoping for Your mercy,
My Lord.

PART TWO

Remember God and He Will Remember You

I Forgot God, and He Made Me Forget Myself!

They said firmly, insistently,
'You must stop, without fail,
Robbing the mighty tyrant
The cover that protects him.
Nay, you have to even sing
The praises of repression, injustice and errantry;
You have to dance
At the festival of the tyranny.

'Write down what we dictate!
State that we disdain,
That we refrain,
To tell the Truth.
Say that we allow
Strikes against Mercy.
Mention that we tolerate
To see justice being whipped.
Do not forget to state that
We will be willing and ready to recognize
The glorification of falsehood.
After all, do not care for anybody.

'But do not forget
To dress up, decorate, and embellish
The swords of injustice,
The daggers of tyranny,
The tools of torture,
And the bullets of murderers
With words, songs, and plays.
This is not something that allows different interpretations!'

'If you do that, we shall forget,
Or seem to forget, all what you have done . . .

Against the revolution.
Remember, and make sure never to forget,
There is a condition:
You must domesticate yourself,
Become one of the disciples of Evil
A weapon of coercion.'

I thought the matter over, considered and deliberated,
And I told myself, stuck in the mud as it was,
'I am willing and I will certainly try
To dance at the festival of tyranny.
I will renounce my faith and my homeland.'

I wrote epics and masterpieces
To glorify inequity and debauchery,
To fly the banners of immorality,
And to paint defeat as victory.
I wiped mercy out of my heart,
And I crossed my name off the dictionary of freedom;
They filled up my quivers
With large sums of money,
So large that my values and ideals just died.

I forgot God, and He made me forget myself.
I affirm that I am bad, that I have perished.
I have become an open field,
In which Satan sows the seeds
Of hatred, apostasy, and atheism,
Slaps the face of justice, reviles all religions,
And madly harvests people like me,
Pushing them down into hellfire.

Death is Just and Inevitable

You, staying put in your burrow,
Come out, have no fear;
To die in the daylight would be
An honour you could be proud of.

You, swimming in a sea of luxury, unaware of anything
   around you,
A day like Doomsday
Is about to come,
Is right at the door-steps.

You, sinking in a bed
Of comfort and ease, of silk and feather,
The nights are bringing
Frost and terrible heat in alteration.

You who read
In the records of the years,
The meanings are confused
Between doubt and certainty.

You, sincere writer, faithful
To the principle of survival and life,
Your papers rise high
To the level of worship and the performance of prayer.

You, asking a human being
For security, for something you need,
The Lord on His Throne
Has decreed the past,
Drawn up the present,
And determined the future.
So you do not have to wonder or be surprised.

O you who wish for

Splendid evenings of dancing,
Bright as suns and moons,
Your eyes betray some doubt
Which robs happy occasions
Of the signs of joy.

You, who are captivated and charmed
By lethal eyelashes,
Your heart must have fallen
Into the seas of shameless eyes.

You, wandering tramp,
Searching for a companion,
Looking for a place to sleep,
Absolute darkness
Is guided by light
To meeting places and camping grounds.

You, shivering and quivering,
And feeling afraid
That the end is near,
Death is inevitable
At the beginning
Or at the end.

My Enemies Dare Not Stand in my Way

My soul would not settle for
Slopes or valleys,
Nor would it put up with
Mountain passes or flood streams;
I belong with seas and oceans,
On mountain tops and summits;
I am a leader
In the deserts, in cities, and in the wilderness;
I am the leader
Of the brave, the bold, and the resolute.

My proud nose
My vigilant mind, my watchful eye,
My broad forehead, my attentive ear,
My loving heart, and pure soil,
And my leaping spirit
Burn flames in me.

Cheating will never be able,
To dissuade me from contemplation and ambition;
I will go on
Along the long and tiring route,
Paying no attention and giving no consideration
To troubles, difficulties and calamities.

My enemies will never be able
To stand in my way:
The elements of nature will defend me;
After all, volcanoes and earthquakes are my father,
Storms, lightning and thunder are my mother,
The brave Naseebah is my wife,
The bright, sharp sword is my brother.
Wild, ferocious beasts

27

Listen to me and obey my command.
Yearning is for me and fear is from me.
Wolves, tigers, and lions
Are my companions and fellow travellers.

I am terror itself, and death is my own spirit;
Fighting is an uncle of mine,
Struggle is another,
And War my grandfather.

If the people call out, urging each other, I shout,
While I am awake, dozing, or asleep,
'I am the fighter in God's service.
God is Great. God is Great.
There is no god but God,
And Muhammad is God's Prophet.'

I have been Very Bold

I said to my son,
'Son, my advice to you is
Not to get married.
Stay as you are,
As I used to be,
Free and unfettered.

'Stay as you are,
As I used to be,
A servant of God,
A prisoner, a husband, for your homeland.

'Stay as you are,
Brave, free,
As I used to be,
In days of old.

My son,
Night has crept in;
Your brothers and sisters are afraid and terrified.
They also are my children.

'I was at a loss,
"Shall I stay at their side?
Or go out to the war
In the darkness of the night?" '

I used to be very bold,
A day gets dark, nights shine with light,
But today I have turned into a coward;
I hesitate, I come up with arguments and excuses
For the sake of the children's eyes.

O my God, O my God,
Is there anything more cruel than a night which, like a rock,

Sits on my chest?
Is there anything more powerful than a morning.
From whose light I hide myself?
O my God, O my God,
I am confused and at a loss.

Shall I let my enemy play around,
Singing his evils?
Shall I let myself be whipped by daytime?
Shall I let myself be hanged at night,
And suffer torture every day?

Shall I die every evening,
And weep and wail
Over a hero who was lost
For the sake of the children's eyes?

'My son,
My advice to you is
Not to get married!'

The Poor Wild Goat is Watching at a Distance

It heavily rained;
My mother called her neighbour,
'Um Hisham,
Listen to the sound of the thunder,
See the flashes of the lightning,
See, Um Hisham,
Flood streams rushing in our desolate valley,
Filling our valley and those of our neighbours.

'Um Hisham,
We have prayed for rain,
We have submissively prayed for rainfalls,
And God has granted our prayers,
So all our pastures bloom and are decorated
With the eyes of jumping, running oryxes,
Which share the feasts with our eyes.

'Um Hisham,
A poor wild goat is watching at a distance:
Hearts have no mercy,
For a mild, friendly animal,
That is more merciful than a deceitful human being
Who has opted for robbery and loves to kill.'

The wild goat felt afraid,
And so did other animals of the forest.
I fell asleep and so did Um Hisham
And all other neighbours,
All but the animals of the forest,
As all of them remain prisoners of fear;
They are worried and uncertain.

Is this right?
Is this fair?
Have no worry, do not be upset,
God is there,
And He is the Most Powerful, the Most Gracious God.

An Insect Devouring a Tree

A billion guileless people repeat
The story of a mean person along the road
Who has claimed to have seen an elephant
In a jug
And an insect devouring a tree,
Walking on two legs,
And storming two mountains
They echo his question about
The dirty pig:
'Who says its meat is unlawful?'

A billion guileless people repeat
The story of a mean person along the road,
But it is enough for the decisive truth
To come out of the lips of a single believer
Who believes in the Only God,
Is only afraid of what is right,
And believes only in telling the truth.
For him world is bound to perish.
Neither money, nor children;
Neither anger, nor approval,
Would deter him from fighting the evils on earth.
He could only be satisfied
When he meets his Lord
With an honourable face
And a kind, merciful heart.

I have Learnt from Life's Patterns

Misgivings have settled in my soul,
Suspicions found a bed in my heart,
And I thought that I shall remain
Throughout life, for ever.

My senses are fine, and they react.
My sight has exceeded miracles.
My hearing has picked up low murmurs and whispers
And has listened to all the sounds of the universe;
It has crossed out from the dictionary
The words of separation, for ever.

My whole being flares up, and my blood boils
With radiance, boldness, and challenge.
My soul subdues tragedies,
Ordering them to wander about and remain unemployed.
My soul forces all my pain and sorrow, and my bitterness
To sleep for ever.

I have learnt from life's patterns
That I am heading towards hardship and misery,
Just as I am healing towards happiness and satisfaction,
Because I am a human being,
Subject to recuperation and to sickness,
Shaken by dreams,
Ready to enjoy the music of hope,
Assassinated by the sharpness of pain, and
Sorrowfully looking to eternity.

Like a child I laugh happily
For days which are to come.
I weep in anguish and distress
Over times that have passed away,
When I used to think
That I will live for ever.

After the sweetness, happiness, and pleasure,
After the bitterness, pain, and misery,
I bear witness that God,
The Lord of the Universe,
Is the One who lives
For ever.

After the sweetness, happiness, and pleasure,
After the bitterness, pain, and misery,
I do bear witness that He is the one-and-only God,
That there is no god but Him,
It is He Who bestows and withdraws power.
He is the Eternal, the Absolute;
'He begetteth not, Nor is He begotten,
And there is none like unto Him.'

Neither Jews nor Christians ...
Neither Muslims nor People
at a Loss

There shall be
Neither whiteness nor blackness,
Neither lines nor ink,
Neither arithmetic nor grammar,
Neither tables nor subjects,
Neither petroleum nor mines,
Neither silver nor gold,
Neither lakes nor springs,
Neither dates nor grapes,
Neither verse nor rhyming phrases,
Neither love nor yearning,
Neither young nor elderly people,
Neither child nor embryo,
Neither universities nor schools,
Neither homeland nor new countries,
Neither gardens nor factories,
Neither beauty nor jewels,
Neither poverty nor wealth,
Neither ugliness nor gloominess,
Neither horses nor race,
Neither sports nor scouting,
Neither wolf nor lamb,
Neither dogs nor lions,
Neither grace nor elegance,
Neither bracelet nor necklace,
Neither shortage nor surplus,
Neither perfection nor immortality,
Neither happiness nor wretchedness,
Neither sociability nor boredom,
Neither need nor necessity,
Neither satisfaction nor discontent,

Neither prose nor conversation,
Neither flood streams nor rain,
Neither security nor peace,
Neither tyrants nor hungry people,
Neither industry nor agriculture,
Neither invention nor pen,
Neither wishes nor contentment,
Neither made-up accusation nor suspicion,
Neither press nor broadcast service,
Neither wars nor revolution,
Neither intimacy nor friendship,
Neither insufficiency nor hospitality,
Neither love nor rendezvous,
Neither pregnancy nor childbirth,
Neither songs nor anything to praise,
Neither clubs nor comrades,
Neither injustice nor debauchery,
Neither submission nor surrender,
Neither hospitals nor medicine,
Neither anesthetics nor tablets,
Neither bullets nor bombs,
Neither withdrawal nor retreat,
Neither attack nor defence,
Neither rockets nor cannons,
Neither prostitution nor immorality,
Neither kernel nor peel,
Neither amity nor friendship,
Neither joy nor pleasure,
Neither pigeons nor swallows,
Neither owls nor vultures,
Neither wise man nor doctor,
Neither reason nor madness,
Neither credit nor banks,
Neither torture nor prisons,
Neither marriage nor wedding,
Neither rejection nor acceptance,
Neither wealth nor children,
Neither violin nor drums,
Neither road nor dams,
Neither mountains nor valleys,
Neither cities nor villages,

Neither kingdoms nor states,
Neither principles nor doctrines,
Neither contradiction nor argument,
Neither Jews nor Christians,
Neither Muslims nor people at a loss,
Neither things nor objects,
Neither voice nor echoes.

The Supreme, the Irresistible will one day, smite
All of these, what is above them,
What is under, and everything else
Within minutes, within seconds,
On 'The Day on which
Every nursing mother
Shall forget the baby she has nursed,
And every pregnant female
Shall drop her load;
You shall see mankind
As in a drunken riot,
Yet not drunk,
But the wrath of God shall be dreadful.'
God, the Almighty, says nothing but the truth.

PART THREE

O My Country
I Shall Redeem You
With My Soul

But Rather a Sword that Beheads Falsehood

My love that goes
Deep into the roots;
My passion which is as firm as mountains;
My high and clear sky;
My lowly, perishable earth;
My cool and fresh air;
My high, dancing palms;
My playful, beautiful brooks;
My distant, bitter waters;
My mysterious, soft sands;
My hot, permanent summer;
My submissive, melancholic autumn;
My misery which lurks in my heart and my soul;
Violent storms of my country;
Evident spring of my country;
Daisy flowers;
Tall and straight figures,
Like minarets, light-houses, and bamboo reeds;
Black and brown hair;
Eyes of the colour of honey;
You, who remember my promise and my pledge;
Festival of the lips, the foreheads and the cheeks;
Wedding-feast full of happiness, the joy, and broad smiles.

Salma, Leila, and Mardhiyah,
Most beautiful maidens on earth,
Sweetest girls of the universe;
Human beings and Jinn of my country;
My strict, tough seriousness;
My innocent, happy playfulness;
My isolated and abandoned amity;
My sleeping, exhausted love;
My still motion;

My violated quiet.

All of these things are in my country,
For in my country I am subject to worries,
As I enjoy happiness and wishes.
In my country, my distress vanishes
When I resort to God, to worship, and to hope.
In my country I never get afraid
Of the evil and corruption.
In my country there is no cheating or fraud,
And there is no hatred, no evil, and no blind submission.

In my country we fight evil;
We make the lords of evil our enemies.
In my country my soul finds rest,
My soul does not think of revolting.
In my country all people
Love one another.
In my country my apprehensions get afraid;
My obstructor trembles and avoids me.
In my country, there are no classes or discrimination,
No guillotines or gallows,
But rather a sword that beheads falsehood.
In my country all people are friends,
Relatives, neighbours and loved ones.
O my relatives, I love you all.
O my country, I shall redeem you with my soul.

We hold Wedding Feasts
for the Faith

In my homeland, in my native city
Among my family and relatives,
I feel safe and secure.
I go through the streets of my city,
Sensing its lanes and alleys,
Shaking hands with friends,
Embracing relatives,
Winking at loved ones,
And greeting strangers.

In my homeland, in my native city,
I am not afraid of tranquillity,
The quiet, or the darkness,
As my native city welcomes every night
Virtuous people and angels,
And expels all devils every night;
It holds wedding-like festivities for Faith,
For Faith retires into it
Like a serpent, retiring into its burrow.
Faith lodges in its heart and bosom.

In my homeland, in my native city,
There is no time for dissimulation,
No place for hypocrisy,
No dwelling for arrogance,
No mansion for tyranny,
No State for falsehood,
And no power for oppression.

In my homeland, in my native city,
The Prophet lived
And died,
And was buried in his own house.

Yet, if you greet him,
He would greet you back.

May the blessings and peace of God be upon you,
The beloved one of God.
May the blessings and peace of God be upon you,
Noblest of His creatures and Messengers,
You, Muhammad, the thankful, the commendable, the
      praiseworthy,
And the trustworthy;
You who are God's mercy for all creatures;
I love you, I love you, I love you,
And love everyone who loves you.
My beloved one, Prophet of God.

So now I am Addicted, Infatuated, and Madly in Love

In my desert, in the wilderness,
My soul is at ease,
Pleased by the sight of wide eyes.
My heart beats in harmony
With sincere hearts.
My bloods run through my body
Like the water of a rivulet irrigating oases.

In my desert, in the wilderness,
My soul is startled
By bold eyes,
Clamorous eyes,
That blow up my soul as the wind blows up soft sand
And blocks the roads to the oases.

In my desert, in the wilderness,
My soul yearns for conversation
With Ghdayer, Munawer, and Badia;
With my grandparents,
My parents, and my friends.

In my desert, in the wilderness,
My courage betrays me,
My sluggishness detains me;
I only see the sand,
The stones, and the drought,
And get surrounded and covered up
By blocks of vacuum.

In my desert, in the wilderness,
My heart does not respond to, or even feel,
The simplicity, the liberality, beautiful women,
The young one, Ghdayer herself,

Who tries to win me gradually,
Determined to hold me captive
To her love and tenderness,
To long-lasting happiness
And short-lived worries.

In my desert, in the wilderness,
My soul is asleep
Unaware of Munawer.
It insists on taking a risk;
It looks for a courageous one,
A renowned person,
That would snatch it and fly away with it
To the highest peak.

In my desert, in the wilderness,
Badia took the initiative;
She winked at me and captured my heart;
She shook up my entire being;
She illuminated the road for me,
And I found out the difference
Between a blazing fire,
And the lights of glittering happiness.
She took me by the hand
To a friendly nest
That does not admit or recognize
Stones or drought,
Nor sands or vacuum.
So now I am addicted, infatuated, and madly in love
With the desert and the wilderness,
And with Badia.

PART FOUR

Bleeding Palestine

I Keep Calling

From Palestine, I call you all,
To tell you, to admit to you,
That I have wished for death,
That I am running down a fatal route;
I have wished to die,
Rather than go on living
In the darkness of injustice –
Rather than go on living in terror
Of an imminent day
When there will be festivities,
.And the devil is invited
To the wedding of Falsehood,
When he will send out invitations to massacres
Beyond the scope of human, or even jinn, imagination.

My brothers, my relatives,
Whoever among you can hear my cries,
I roar, I shout,
I yell out of pain
Greater than any pain, than the worst imagined pain.
I yell out of a pain
Which no doctor can treat,
No physician can heal,
And no prescription can cure.
It is a pain with which
Neither the charms of witch-doctors
Nor the drugs of unbelievers
Can do any good.

My brothers, my relatives,
Whoever among you can hear my cries,
I am shouting in a valley
Which has no echoes,
A valley which the enemies
Have overtaken.

I shout and cry
Out of a pain which was conceived
In the belly of injustice
And was born out of the womb of bitterness.

The Palestinian and the Enemy

No, no one will be able
To keep me from telling the truth;
No one will be capable
Of forcing me to do what is wrong.
I will not be tricked with bitter honey
In which poison is mixed.
I will ignore all statements,
All acts of deception which follow hinted promises.
No I will not shut up;
I will not keep quiet
About what has been done.
No inadvertent silence could make me mute,
And no ignorant uproar will dissuade me.

I will reveal all the secrets,
Uncover what the curtains are hiding,
Blow up all dams and obstacles,
And demolish all walls and fences,
And with my tears I will dissolve my afflictions,
And with my blood wash off my sins.
My slogan will be:
'No afflictions, no sins, and no shame.'

I hear sirens
Which announce, while my body roasts on fire,
That you are conspiring
To liquidate me, then make a statement
That I am both the hangman and the victim;
To describe and delineate me
As both the slanderer and the scandal;
To make me, in very emphatic terms,
The murderer and the murdered.

You did not,
Do not,

And will not know me;
I shall argue and dispute;
I shall resist and fight;
I shall accuse you of lying,
Meanness, and desecration;
I shall accuse you of consulting
Tyrants, as well as Satan himself.

I shall put you on trial and have as witnesses for the prosecution
Abraham and Moses,
Aaron and Isaac,
Solomon and Jacob,
And Sheba and Hajar.
And I shall sentence you to ... happiness
In the valley of misery;
I shall throw you into a dusty prison,
Where food is coal-hot stones,
Water is red blood,
And life is
Drudgery, wretchedness, affliction,
And extinction.

I Almost Forgot the Three Females

I am an Arab from Palestine,
From Gaza,
My father was imprisoned by the Jews.
They assassinated him, taking him by surprise.
He is survived by seven boys
And three girls.

I am going to tell you a story,
The story of the seven boys
And three girls,
And what they have been through
Since the calamity.

The first one went to Cairo,
Got an education, became a master of patience,
Married an Egyptian Muslim lady,
Who was very religious, shy and patient.

The second one migrated to Kuwait.
He did business, struggled, and braved death.
Now he is rich
And supports the family.

The third one travelled to the Honoured City of Makkah,
And paid homage to the Prophet of God
In Medina, the City of Light.
He yearned, while greeting God's Prophet,
For the Noble City of Quds.
He toured the settled lands of Islam,
So now he has a clear vision,
And a strong and unrelenting faith.
Now he is firm and steadfast;
No enemy can invade his lair.

The fourth one is an excellent boy;

He knows both sides of all questions. He checks
     the buyer and the seller.
And he talks only when necessary.

As for the fifth one,
He is the like of the sixth:
Handsome, generous, smiling,
Friendly, easy to like, good-humoured,
A person who pays no attention to evil
And is not afraid of prison,
Like his brothers in Gaza, Haifa, Yafa and Quds,
Like the steadfast fighters in Nablus
And all over Palestine.

I almost forgot the three females.
The first is now a doctor,
A scientist, a famous person.
The second is a revolutionary;
She roars like ferocious lions,
As for the third one,
She is like me;
She runs in the streets,
Fighting with stones.

A Hydrogen Bomb

Shamir and Sharon surely
Watch television.
They must be following
The news of the occupied territories and of all Palestine,
And witnessing what is happening
To Erza, Golda and Cohen.

They get angry and flare up;
They blame Palestinian mothers,
They blame the shots of guns
And they blame canons and machine-guns
How, yes how,
Do they fail to hit
The wombs of Palestinian women.

Shamir hits the table with his fist,
And Sharon releases rotten gasses
Out of his dirty stomach;
They say,
'We have killed thousands!
How and where from have they come back,
Proudly flashing at our faces
Signs of victory
And casting stones at us?'

They say with impudence,
'We have slaughtered with our four hands,
And tortured with our twenty fingers,
All the men and women, old people,
Children and young women of Palestine.
Shylock, Menachem, and Shariat
Have participated in the torture and killing,
And so have Rachel and even prostitute Meir
And all the "chosen" people.
We have left no farmer or caretaker

Or village chief on the soil of Palestine.

'How do they come back?
Where do they come back from,
These rebellious children
Who throw stones
And carry the flag of Palestine.

'It is inevitable, it is unavoidable, that we should declare
General mobilization.
We must appeal for help
To both the living and the dead.
Where are Shemon and Rabin?
Where are Golda and Ben Gurion?
Where is Menachem?
Where is Moshe Dayan?

'No, we have no use
For common methods,
Nor the employment of traditional weapons.
It is inevitable that we should use
An atomic bomb.'

Every Palestinian mother replies,
From inside and outside,
From the most remote corner in Palestine,
'My womb, yes, my womb
Is a hydrogen bomb.'

God is my All-Sufficient Patron

My mouth is shut, closed up,
Full of stones,
The same as the stones of Palestinian children.
Palestinian children stones today
Silence all writers and poets.
There is no doubt that Palestinian children
Are the writers, the poets,
Who are writing epics,
Superior to all folk epics,
And they compose poems
Superior to all the poems
Of poet laureates.

They come up with expressions,
And discover rhymes,
Known and comprehended only by those
Who are care-laden,
Beaten, robbed of their arms;
Whose arms and legs were broken
By Zionists and they were made to bleed;
Whose blood drops and bone splinters
Are all over Palestine.

My son who flies
To the soft breeze of paradise,
My martyred son,
Dweller of the valleys of paradise –
My daughter, my honour,
Who are more precious
Than the lives of all my enemies –
My son and my daughter,
I have fought, am fighting, and will ever fight
The scum of the earth,
The enemies of God,
Who have planted sorrow in my land,

57

In my soil and in my heart.
So let the winds of my fury
Uproot the trees, houses, and symbols of the usurper;
Let the entire world
Be rocked, shaken, collapsed and destroyed.
And I shall spit out my mouthful
Of dust, sand, and stones,
And I shall speak up and tell –
I shall accuse the entire world, all humanity,
With whatever words I may have;
I shall accuse even my own brother
And affirm that my brother is a traitor,
Squandering funds in a world of illusion
And undertakes such acts
As violate the codes of chivalry
So that he may become a leader and stand above
My humiliation, on a heap of my own bones
And on the dreads that I have suffered.

They say in America and Europe,
'Elect and choose!'
Who – whom should I choose?
No, I shall choose
My brother, nor my cousin,
Nor the neighbour.
I shall rely on myself
And I shall repeat at all times,
'God is my all-sufficient patron;
He is the best one to trust in.'

PART FIVE

Me?
Who Am I?

I Am an Obedient Servant
of God's

Is it said that I am a false lover?
That I am a confused, madly-in-love person?
That I pay money
To buy love?
That I am unbearable?
That I am always the one to be blamed,
The one who has fabricated,
Bargained, sold, and bought?

It is said I don't enjoy chords and notes,
And I am not moved by books or pens.
They say I am awkward and stupid,
A double-crosser and a vagabond,
That I will beg
And become one of the hungry lot,
And that I will slip down no doubt
To the rock bottom.

It is said that I am an imbecile?
A drunkard?
A lunatic?
All of these are said about me,
All what was and is said.

In fact, I am not like that,
I am the opposite of this, the contrary image of that.
I am not entertained by hypocrisy,
Troubled by dissimulation,
Visited by feelings of fear,
Or living close to worries and concern.

Then, who am I?
I am an obedient servant of God's

A captive servant
For the Creator.
I shall forget everyone who has talked.
Let them say more, those who are going to speak.
About my stupidity and my atrocities;
My misfortune, my misery and my tribulation;
My cross temper, my loneliness and my alienation –
God is the greatest of all,
The greatest to Whom all submit,
The greatest to Whom all yield,
The greatest to Whom all surrender,
The greatest Whom all obey and
To Whom all are loyal.

I Am an Extremist who has Deviated

Between you and me
Is the proverbial hair of Mu'awiyah;
I know this single hair,
I have tested it, and I have learned
To relax my hold if you pull.
How about you, what will you do?
If I draw it, if I pull it,
Will you relax your hold?

Between the two of us
There is admiration, love, and affection
On my part,
And you do respond
To my affection, love, and admiration,
With a cunning hair;
You gradually draw me to a neutral zone.

I hate this single, fine hair,
Which I hardly see.
I blame myself for having learnt
How to pull and how to relax.
I have arrived at a decision;
I will have any dealings with this single hair,
Which is the corner-stone and foundation
In all manoeuvres and the game of politics,
And, quite frankly, I am not
Well-versed in manoeuvres,
And I hate politics.

I am an extremist who has deviated;
I am fed up with equilibrium and neutrality;
I have been swept to the farthest end of separation;
I have thrown myself and ended up

In the heart of torture;
As I do not agree
To remain neutral,
Like Mu'awiyah's hair;
I must either be in sweet happiness
Or in bitter misery.

I affirm, I insist and I am positively sure
That I must choose and find the difference
Between paradise and hell,
And not remain neutral,
Like the proverbial hair of Mu'awiyah.

I Love up to Death

An active volcano is in my heart,
An atomic bomb is in my soul,
And there is, in my mind, thoughts that urge me
To forget the volcano
And to neutralize the atomic bomb.

Yet, I am a human being,
And I hate and love,
Without consulting my mind.
I hate and love
By the authority of my heart;
My love and hatred
Are not subject to
Calculations and statistics.

I love up to death
And hate up to the demise of the death,
And this is something dictated
By my soul and my heart.

What shall I do with my soul and heart,
When my mind is overcome by whims?
I am an infatuated person,
Seduced by love
And conquered by
Mad hatred.

I Have Regained my Self-Confidence

I am a relative of the one who struck,
And a partner of the one who looted;
I get away and forget,
But scabs cover my body again and keep after me.
I am in an impossible condition, a wonder of wonders.

My pillars get demolished;
Flames burn bright in my heart;
My whole being shakes;
Fury gets ablaze in my soul.

I do not covet and do not want
Eminence, riches, or titles.
My laziness, submission, and servility have dried up.
My dependence on others has been reversed.
My apprehension is dormant.
My fear is itself afraid; it has run away.

I have regained my self-confidence.
And have I forgotten? I see my yesterday,
My feeble voice, my rare whispers,
My surrender and my trembling,
My impudence, stupidity and submissiveness,
The shivers of my disgrace, compliance, and atrocity,
And my waiting for this day.

It is a day I shall never forget,
A day on which I have regained myself,
The day of amity and dignity,
A new and a clean day,
The day of happiness, joy and pride,
Just like my wedding day.

How can my Life go on Without Resonance?

I sail and go deep into water,
I swim against the tide,
I resist the overpowering current;
Seconds, minutes and hours betrayed me.
And numerous, countless, gloomy
And lost days let me down
And so did long and empty distances.

My hope ridiculed me,
My goal moved away from me.
I left my companions,
My family members quarrelled with me,
And my neighbour turned into an enemy of mine.

They consulted one another and said,
'You are acting against your interests.'
They began to whisper,
Backbiting and gossiping,
Forgetting me and having a good time together,
Forgetting me and dancing,
Then they would recover and remember,
Repeat things and tell lies,
And give orders with an air of conceit and arrogance, 'Bend your
    head to the storm;
Bow in submission to important people.'

No I shall never bend my head to storms,
No, nor shall I ever bow in submission to important people.
How can I abandon my knowledge and learning?
How can I forget my generosity and tolerance?
How can I deform my radiance?
How can I spoil my perfume?
How can I accept and approve of

Being chewed up and spit
By the current of ignorance, the tide of tartars?

How can my life go on without resonance?
How can I forget my family and country, and my yearning?
How can I accept to be shaped by my enemies
Into a frightened gem,
That sleeps on chests,
Indifferent and immobile?

What do you want?
What do you have in mind?
Do you want me to swim,
To sail with the current?
Do you think I will walk about
Without an identity or number?
Would you be satisfied with my destruction?
Would you be content with my loss?
In the tumult of the sea?
Without any ports or harbours,
To be imprisoned by the chief traitor,
Who would torture me, crush me, reject me,
And then drop me, with great stupidity,
In the desert or on a coast,
Unable to hear or feel,
Without any vision or any life,
And hang on my chest
A medal of cheating and falsehood, or of tin,
And adorn my head with a crown
Of hypocrisy, flattery and frost?

It is true that I do sail
In the seas of despair,
And true that I fight the currents
And the fits of hopelessness,
True that I do swim
In lakes of wretchedness
Against all currents
Of inflexibility and unjust accusations,
Without a weapon and without conditions.

Since my oars were broken,
My companion committed suicide,
And my vessel exploded
Among the storms and afflictions and in the midst of conspiracy,
I resist and fight
And wrestle with the tide and the waves,
And I do not care if I die.

But, I do care to die
Standing up and erect,
Like the milestones and monuments,
As a symbol of obstinacy, challenge,
Opposition and steadfastness,
With faith that God is one.

Pens Have Hit the Bottom of Ignominy

No, I shall not relinquish
What I believe in;
No, I shall not board a ship sailing
To a degraded port, infested with pestilence.

I am an Arab Muslim
Not a chauvinist, addicted
To blond, red, or yellow smoke.
I am not a detested separatist,
Or a hated bawdy man,
Who openly commits his shameful deeds,
And boasts, on every occasion.
Of prostitution;
Appeals to ignorance,
The ignorance of Muhammad's infidel uncle;
Or promotes the principles of
A dingy, imbecile atheist,
Who is much worse than a dirty pig,
A rotten old goat,
Or a scabied dog.

Certain ideas have been driven away,
And hired and submissive pens
Have hit the bottom of ignominy.
In the land of Islam
Banners have been flying high,
The flags of this religion,
The flags of the enemies of polytheism,
The flags of the foes of atheists
And of all human beings and Jinn who have lost their way,
Lost the route of mercy,
Turned away from Al-Kowther,
And lost paradise.

We Leave Something for Love

I don't believe, nor am I convinced,
That dwelling place of love is the heart;
When I surrender, it is to a woman, both beautiful and
    intelligent.
I root for the mind.

My mind moves my heart, not the other way round.
It imposes through thinking and strategy
Hatred or love.
Forcing it to go far,
Or ordering it to get near.

My heart has been moved by a living statue,
Carved out of the backbone of loveliness,
Stamped and sealed with perfection.
It said to me, 'Try!'
My heart spoke to my mind
About a conceited statue which struts
With one foot boasting, the other playing haughty,
And between the two feet, I am at a loss,
Because of their anger and quarrel,
Their hot competition and jealousy.

One foot ridicules the other,
'I hold the most beautiful branch of a tree.
I named it the branch of splendour.'
The other gets angry and jealous, and says,
'Without me, you cannot
Stagger, jump, or even move;
You cannot sway or strut.'

My mind whispered to my heart pointing out
How the verdict shall be prisoner
In the bottom of a well.
So my heart spoke in secret,

But very clearly,
And did not pay attention to the contention of the two feet.
It described, in detail,
What was between the two, the madness of the two.
It pledged to keep secret.
What my two lips would do to the two lips.
It said, 'Your decision is
What the two eyes may expose.'
An eyebrow was liften in surprise,
And the strokes of whips came
Out of an eyelash that was trying to avoid
An invasion of the mind.
It was conspiring, insisting on invading the heart.

After some minutes, or say few hours,
All bodies were seen as equal
By the mind.
The parties of the false love
Disbanded in cool pleasure.
And an important, crucial decision
Was issued by my two eyes.

My mind is preoccupied,
And my soul longs for
Arguments and conversation.
My mind is looking for any girl
Who may charm my mind
And give birth to males and females,
Sprung from my loins;
Who reads books and writes poetry,
As well as prose, and sneaks into my soul.
For my love could not be renewed,
And my mind could not be inflamed,
By any girl other than a wise and beautiful one,
Who snatches my mind away,
Settles in my soul,
And leaves something for love.

My Soul is Refreshed by a Particular Memory

And an old man gets busy with his lute,
Hitting the strings,
Playing the instrument
Again and again.

Evoking ancient tunes for inspiration,
Appealing to old days for help,
His fingers tremble,
As the heart does,
His eyes sink deep,
His eyebrows droop
And the pulse of the heart
Sheds tears for the memory.

That's how I have been
Since boyhood, my spirit
Gets intoxicated
With old tunes,
And my soul is refreshed by a particular memory,
Looking forward to the arrival, the homecoming,
So that it may sleep in the bossom of dreams.

My heart beats and dances
To the notes of beautiful tunes.
An old man gets busy with his lute,
An old man who plays the strings
Again and again,
Shouting, singing, and having fun,
For everybody is intoxicated
By the music of his tunes.

They Sleep under the Dust,
in a Grave

They said, 'Your poetry is not a good material
For singing and music.
The composer is trying, having some trouble,
And the singer is mute, unable to utter a word,
Looking at a lute that suffers great difficulty,
Like a pregnant woman,
Exhausted by the hours of labour,
And can give birth only through a caesarean operation.'

I replied, 'I have recited no poetry,
Nor did I read any poems
Or invent new words and expressions.
In what I write, I describe marvels
Which sink and settle down, living through time,
Passed on from generation to generation,
And relayed by grandchildren quoting their grandmothers.'

And also said many other things:
'I have no interest in composers and singers,
Nor in choruses of men and women;
They are all mortal and transient.
I am proud that what I say and write,
Has been too difficult to be accompanied by music
And too difficult for singers to sing.'

They said, 'There are, in your words
The notes of a tune, or an overture,
That flatters the spirit and the soul,
And tickles the ego and the id.
You drown in narcissism
And intently and premeditatedly play
The hymn of insolence and arrogance.

Without knowing it, you sing
A song drenched in vanity.'

I said, 'I beg your pardon,
I am no versifier and no poet.
I hate to be a versifier,
And I fear being a poet.
For some poets of this age
Are false and lying witnesses,
And all the versifiers of this time of ours
Are superficial and inferior.
Most epics of this period
Sleep under the dust, in a grave
And would not be recited in the camps or palaces.
The masterpiece poems of these times
Have dropped into stagnant water,
Which can never produce
Any flowery poems.

'I am only a messenger, capable of error,
With a message from prose to poets,
Addressing them, saying,
"You have done a bad job, both in content and form,
And your poetry has turned out like white powder,
Like heroin or opium,
Like a black day."

'If my words are a flame,
And my letters are blazing with anger,
And if the first one among you have run away,
Your last one have been infested with scabies,
And the majority of you belong to looting tribes
Recite scum poems
And write obscene fabrications –
My knowledge, my forbearance,
My patience, my silence,
My lines, my prose and my poetry
Are all made of gold.'

PART SIX

I Love You, I Love You,
I Love You, Beloved Prophet of God

You Are My Loved One and the
Loved One of Every Lover

When I think of you
And hear even one letter of your name,
I dream of the perfection of that name
And I am filled with satisfaction and pleasure.

I see hope,
As clearly as I see the sun and the moon.
I feel happy,
Tranquil, calm, and peaceful.

When I remember that you will be present
On the day of need, the Day of the Gathering,
'The Day whereon neither wealth
Nor sons will avail,'
'The Day thou shalt see mankind
As in a drunken riot, yet not drunk,'
I say, at the top of my voice
To this mortal world,
This transient universe,
That you are my first love
And my last love,
That you will intercede for those who worship
And spend the night in pious prayers.

You are my loved one and the loved one of every lover,
Whether silent or loud,
Whether a sinner or a repentant person,
Whether charitable and generous
Or an inadvertent miser.

I love you, my master, Muhammad,
Of the Hashem family,
I love you, I love you, I love you,

And I love those who love you,
Beloved Prophet of God.

80

Your Name is Carved in My Conscience

The heart weeps,
The eye sheds tears,
Memories make one bleed,
Thoughts cause wounds,
And all are bound to be forgotten.

But you,
And only you,
Are absent and present,
Absent, hiding in my conscience,
Deep inside my heart,
And present in my wakefulness,
In my consciousness and my mind.

You, who could not be forced out of my sight
By events and adventures,
And could not be erased out of my thoughts
By neither grief nor joy.

You! You are the one permanently stamped
In the heart and in the mind,
Your name is carved in my inner conscience,
A frequent name on my tongue.
Everybody shall know of my love,
My passionate, ardent love.

I shall travel to all countries
And meet children,
Women, and men;
And I shall shake hands with them,
One by one,
And each of them will know
That I am head over heels in love,

My beloved Prophet of God,
My intercessor, whom God loves.

May the blessings of God be upon you,
May the angels send blessings to you,
We send you our blessing on and salute and bless you.
I love you, I love you, I love you,
And love all who love you,
Beloved Prophet of God.

May God's Blessing Be Upon You

The full moon rose
Beauty covered the whole universe,
Light spread out
In all directions, over the horizons,
Grace disrobed and perfection stood erect,
Necks, foreheads, and bodies bowed,
And the grass and trees trembled,
And calmness, quiet, and expectation
Prevailed in jungles and forests.

Nightingales sang,
The desert bloomed,
Sands danced in joy,
And beautiful maidens
Walked, praising God,
In submission, saluting and saying, 'God is great.'
An embryo in the uterus
Muttered and repeated,
'There is no god but God;
Muhammad is the Prophet of God.'

How about happy grey pigeons?
They flew up, conversing intimately,
Moving far and near in happiness.
And flowers and roses?
Flowers sighed
And smiled, and roses laughed.

How about diligent ants?
They all stood still
From morning till sunset.
And blessed bees?
It buzzed and soared, accompanying in rhythm
The dancing tunes.

How about little sparrows?
How come they are leaping and jumping,
Indifferent to the great hunter.
They have seen lions
Sleep, ignoring a host of prey.

And hungry wolves?
Wolves have reached a reconciliation
With the flock
And with trembling gazelles?
Gazelles have become intimate
With tigers.
And rapacious vultures?
They smiled
At rabbits and the birds?
And the spotted viper?
What made the spotted viper
Refrain from its habitual killing?

And loud thunder?
The thunder jested with
The clouds.
And blasting winds?
They were transformed
Into gentle breeze.
And the high mountains?
The mountains were forgiving
With plains and rocks
And the torrential floods?
They were lenient
With hillocks and summits.

The anxious Caesar,
Why doesn't he sleep?
While Chosroe, in his luxury,
Woke up
From his dream, from his comfort,
With his heart beats
And his sweat drops
Accelerating in fear.

This universe woke up
To a new, unique dawn.
Poor people,
Orphans, and slaves all chanted,
'This is the new morning.
This is the true promise.
This is the happy Eid.'

The day of the light dawned,
A day which the Most Gracious, Most Compassionate,
Selected
For his chosen one to be born,
So that faith would prevail,
And fire be extinguished.

My vigilant mind,
My pure soul,
My permanent joy,
My ardent passion,
My fragrant perfume,
My sober breath,
My heart, deep in love,
With the true Guide, Muhammad,
The best of all who passed away,
The best of all who came,
And the last of all who may come with a message.

May the blessing of God be on you,
The universe, with all those who are in it, send
Their blessings to you,
My master, my loved one,
Muhammad.
I love you, I love you, I love you,
And love all who love you,
Beloved Prophet of God.

You Are the Handsomest Baby Ever to Come Out of a Womb

I

'And you have an exalted standard of character.'
You are the one who swims, is drowned, in luxury,
On the hillsides of paradise,
In the valleys of the eternal life,
And you are the chosen one, the thankful one,
The selected one, the commendable one,
Purity and clarity,
A gem radiant with light
In every place, at all times,
Your name is written and engraved
The Throne Supreme,
You are the one God loves,
Beloved Prophet of God.

II

When God, the Initiator and Reiterator desired
To praise and commend you,
He did not say you were intelligent, valient
Courageous, bold,
Sagacious,
Leading, or victorious;
Or you were a king
Or a chief.
He, Who is Full of Majesty, rather said,
'And you have an exalted standard of character.'
Beloved Prophet of God.

III

Do you want safety?
Do you want salvation?
Do you want a way out of a plight?
And do you want a spacious grave?

And do you want to get rid off
The spectre of an ugly devil?
And do you want a mansion in paradise?
Then, follow Muhammad, and the example he set,
And be like Muhammad, as he is described by God:
'And you have an exalted standard of character.'
Beloved Prophet of God.

IV

The chosen Prophet walked
On thorns. He walked,
Suffered, and travelled. He walked
In the quest of mercy for mankind,
Soliciting forgiveness for mankind.
He was never filled with despair by man's obstinacy;
He was never afraid of the length of the distance.
He rather tried, did his best, persevered,
And declared to all people statement which said,
'I have been sent so as to bring moral standards to perfection.'
'And you have an exalted standard of character,'
Beloved Prophet of God.

V

God, Who is the one and only God, addressed
All messengers and prophets, other than him,
From Adam to Jesus by their names.
Yes, you were the exception, you, giver of good tidings,
Who are loved by the Almighty,
My loved one,
My intercessor.
He spoke of you and to you
As the Prophet, the Messenger,
The master of all creatures,
The first and last of messengers and prophets.
He said that Islam was your religion and your message,
And the religion of all messengers and prophets.
He said that you were an abundant store of provisions,
A universal bounty;
That your grandfather was Abraham, father of prophets;
That Moses and Jesus were led in prayers by you,
And so did all messengers and prophets,

Praying to the Primal Originator, the Everlasting and Self-
    Subsisting,
Whom 'No slumber nor sleep can seize,'
God, God, the Great One,
Who said about you,
'And you have an exalted standard of character.'
Beloved Prophet of God.

VI

Man with a bright smile,
With cheerfulness and pleasant temper,
With generous acts,
With noble feet,
Compiler of all miracles,
Between the lines, between the pages,
In a single Sacred Volume,
Where in every verse that it has,
There is a supernatural miracle, nay miracles.
Man with a noble character,
God describes you in His Book and says,
'And you have an exalted standard of character.'
Beloved Prophet of God.

VII

The darkness of night brightened,
Day spread all over the darkness,
The superstitions of unbelievers broke up,
And the dams of the lecherous collapsed
On the day Orphan Muhammad was born,
He was a bright lantern which shone up.
The legions of the absolute truth marched on
Under the leadership of Muhammad, the trustworthy,
Defeater of darkness and of utter falsehood.
You are blessed with light, the light of perfection,
God, the Most Supreme, Perfect in Knowledge, described
    you and said:
'And you have an exalted standard of character.'
Beloved Prophet of God.

VIII

From you perfume borrows its scent,
Beauty embellishes itself with your beauty,
Loveliness surrenders to your brightness.
You wore the cleanest, most elegant clothes
And let your hair down to the lobes of your ears;
You took a bath, perfumed yourself, and applied kohl to your
    eyes:
You are the handsomest baby ever to come out of a womb
'And you have an exalted standard of character,'
Beloved Prophet of God.

IX

Some reporters who fabricate stories say,
'Don't be happy! Don't enjoy yourselves!
Don't sing! Don't smile!
You are only on a short trip.'
We say, 'Yes, true,
But do not ignore the gift with which the Benefactor has blessed
    us,
Nor what the Source of Peace, the Primal Originator, has created,
Such as trees, flowers, and cattle;
Such as the agreement, concord, and harmony!
Don't you enjoy the singing of the birds
In spring and in autumn?
Don't you enjoy colours, leaves, and flowers!
Ask yourselves! Ask your hearts!
Aren't you infatuated with charming figures?
Aren't you captivated by the silk-like hair?
Don't your hearts beat at the blinking of an eyelash?
Don't you find the quiver of some eyelid breathtaking?
Aren't you held prisoners by the eyes of the gazelle?
Aren't you intoxicated by the wine of perfection?
Don't you ever accept God's charity?
Didn't you read the life story of Beloved Muhammad,
The handsome, the man with grace, to whom elegance belongs?
'And you have an exalted standard of character.'
Beloved Prophet of God.
Beauty yielded to your radiance,
Elegance slept on your eyelids,
And ugliness was defeated by your birth.

You drank to satisfaction lawful, fresh and pure water,
Which flows in the eyes and faces,
In bodies and chests, and over lips.
Master of all creatures, ideal embodiment of moral standards,
'You have an exalted standard of character.'
Beloved Prophet of God.

XI

Your message has been and still is
The happiness of all creatures, all people,
In this banal, perishable world
And in the happy, everlasting Hereafter.
You never betrayed any one, even your enemies.
You called out and told them,
When in full victory and having the upper hand,
'Go, for you are free!'
You turned people of different races into brothers.
You said more than once,
'None of you shall be a good believer
Before he loves, for his brother, what
He loves for himself.'
For you drums were beaten
By the virgins of good Taiba,
Along the road, in the fields.
The virgins of good Taiba
Were happy at your arrival,
So they sang along your route,
'The moon has risen for us
Out of the folds of Al-Wada' mountains.
We are thus bound to express our thanks,
Every time someone prays to God.'
'And you have an exalted standard of character.'
I love you! I love you! I love you!
And I love all who love you,
Beloved Prophet of God.

The Day of Fear and Disunion

We were away from our home country,
And it was Friday,
The day of rest and pleasure
At home.

A television channel covered
The Friday prayer
From the most beloved spot in the world.
The Friday speaker stood up
At the Mosque of God's Prophet,
Teaching us about, reminding us of,
The day of Migration,
The day of fear
And of happiness.

The speaker prayed for God's blessing for the Elect Messenger.
We did the same, again and again,
Praying for the man God loves.
On Fridays, it is recommended
To keep on praying for the blessings of God
For our loved one, the chosen one,
The last of God's prophets,
The thankful, the praiseworthy one,
The first and the last of all prophets.

You, who are handsome and of the highest moral standards,
Tolerant and kind,
Obedient to God,
Humble before God,
Much dearer to me than my own self –
I love you! I love you! I love you,
And love all who love you,
Beloved Prophet of God.

91

Why Do We All Love You?

No one and nothing would dissuade me
From this love,
For I love you and everybody loves you,
And I love you to the utmost limit of your love,
And even beyond it.
And in order to reach what is above
The climax of your love,
I love your love,
In your love to the ultimate dimension of your love.

Love in the morning,
Love at noon,
Love in the afternoon,
Love in the evening,
Love in-between morning and noon,
Love in-between noon and the afternoon,
Love in-between the afternoon and evening,
And love in-between every love and the next.

Why do we all love you?
Because your love is wide, big, and great.
I feel that I, alone,
Feel this love for you.
Yet every one who loves you feels
That he comes first
In this love.

Your love, beloved one,
Is ultimate love.
Seat of affection in my heart,
Light of my reason,
Lantern of my eyesight,
Radiance of my insight,
And springtime of my desert –
I love you! I love you! I love you!

I love you, Muhammad,
Son of Abdullah.
I love you beyond the most distant
Horizons of all love.
May the blessing of God be upon you,
Angels, human beings, and jinn all pray
For God's blessings for you.
I love you, and love you, and love you,
And I love all who love you,
Beloved Prophet of God.

He was Subject to the Overbearing One

My master whom I love, Muhammad,
Was a messenger, a Prophet, and a human being,
An orphan, illiterate person, who hoped for and solicited
    forgiveness.
He used to be afraid, to tremble;
He used to ask and solicit
Mercy from the Most Merciful,
Miracles from One All-Knowing,
The favour of the Most Generous One
And the love of the Loved One.

He submitted to the Overbearing One,
And was humble before the Supreme.
His constant concern was God, who is the highest
Watcher and Investigator.

He had companions whom he used to teach,
To consult with, and to fight along with them.
Honest Abubakr
Was the friend of the Prophet of God,
And he has become the Caliph who succeeded God's Prophet.
He was a steadfast person,
An arbiter,
A steel dam
That stopped apostates.

As for Omer, the sage,
I find no expressions which can do him justice,
And neither poems,
Nor prose novels could assist me,
In describing that giant.
Who used to become smaller and smaller,
And his tears used to flow,
His limbs used to tremble at the thought of injustice,
And willingly he submitted to justice.

94

I wonder! I am surprised!
How could tears flow out of Omer's eyes?
How could he feel afraid,
He, who was assured that he had a guaranteed place in paradise?
But the All-Knowing, All-Divine,
Always made him live
In fear, in anxiety,
So that he may serve as a lesson and an example
For the human beings and jinn,
And all creatures.

Now, what shall I tell you
About you, about myself, and about the difference
Between yesterday's mountains and summits
And today's mountain feet and lowlands?

Can any of you
Reach the summits of the Honest One?
Or the heights of the Arbiter?
It is as if I don't believe
That the Honest One and the Arbiter
Were human beings like me and you.

These two lights!
The truthful, Honest One,
And the just Arbiter,
The first being the companion at the Cave,
And the second a Prophet
If there could have been one after Muhammad,
That was what Muhammad said.
May the blessings of God be upon him.
The peace of God and His angels
And of mankind and jinn be upon him.
I love him! I love him! I love him,
And I love all who love him.
Beloved Prophet of God.

From the Notebooks of My Daughters

I read in my daughters' notebooks.
Rotana wrote,
'The longest word is eternity.'
Well done, Rotana,
Native of palm-tree land!
Well done, Rotana,
Daughter of the person whom the Prophet for all creatures, God's
     Prophet,
Recommended to be well treated.
Well done, because eternity is long,
Very, very long,
And you are the ample good.
Yes my child, my little one,
You are just a small, tiny part,
Yet you have discovered, at such an early age,
That the end is either paradise or hell.

Arawa jotted down,
'The fastest word is time,'
O my dear Arawa
Let me drink to satisfaction, as your name implies,
And then make me drink again,
Seat of affection in my heart;
Extinguish my fire and let me drink
The light of your look,
The grace of your form,
The beauty, the purity,
Inside you, in your inner self.
I named you, my dear,
After the aunt of God's Prophet.

Nasibah made some scribbles; she wrote
On walls, on paper,
'The sweetest word is homeland.'
Nasibah, you are close to my heart.

I have votively offered you, my dear,
To the homeland and the Faith.
And you, my dear, are named after
She who defended the most noble creature,
The Prophet of God,
Your namesake was praised
And commended by the purest of all creatures,
The Messenger of God.
And you, my dear, will fight
For Al Quds, Makkah, and Medina.

Amina affirms and insists that
'The sweetest name is Muhammad.'
O Amina, namesake of the mother of the loved one,
You are bounty and the act of giving,
You are paradise for remote people,
And a spring for those near.
How did you know, my little one,
How did you discover, with your limited knowledge,
That the sweetest of all names
Is the name Muhammad?
On the day I choose for you
The same name as my paradise, my mother,
My grief committed suicide, my worries were drowned.

Fatima, the youngest of the bunch,
Is solidified honey, unavailable honey,
She indicates and points out,
Without speaking,
Without uttering a word,
That 'the greatest word is God.'
There is no god but God;
Muhammad is God's Prophet.
O Fatima, my sweet,
Take your Book and recite the Holy Quran,
For from every one of its verses,
And of its chapters,
The light of eloquence shines and radiates.

Fatima, daughter of the Prophet;
O Fatima, mother of Al-Hassan and Al-Hussein,

Ali's wife, the Prophet's daughter,
You are guided by three lights:
You are born from the loins of the trustworthy Prophet, the guide
   to the right way;
You are an example of good behaviour
And you are a miracle for the world.
Among women you represent
Modesty, generosity, and succour.
You are the daughter of my beloved one.
You are the daughter of the man God loves,
God's Prophet,
Master of mankind, of all prophets and messengers.
May the blessing and peace of God
Be upon the best of God's creatures,
Muhammad, His Prophet.
I love him! I love him! I love him!
And I love all who love him.
Beloved Prophet of God.

I Have a Son Named Like You, Muhammad

I was walking along the seaside avenue,
Inhaling the sea breeze,
Without a companion or friend;
I was swimming in sea air,
Recalling with every step I took
The steps of Dawn,
As he walked slowly,
Closing the doors of night,
And opening the doors for light.

I turned my memory back to the most sacred spot,
At a time I was a child,
And did not comprehend or grasp
That I loved next door to the Prophet,
That I walked on a soil
Upon which the Prophet of God had walked,
That I ate the dates of a palm-tree,
Of which Abubakr and Omer had eaten,
That I drank the same water
Of which the Leader of all God-fearing people had drunk,
And that I lived
In the land most loved by God.

I was walking
And in front of me, a child,
Small as I once was, was walking;
He blocked my way and said,
'The sea is beautiful; the sea is big.'
Then, he started to throw pebbles into the sea.

I asked him, 'What is your name?'
He said, 'Muhammad.'
I said, 'I have a son whose name is Muhammad, like yours;

My father also named my brother Muhammad.
Another brother of mine has only one son, who is Muhammad.
A third brother has two sons, one of whom is Muhammad.
My fifth brother also named one of his sons Muhammad.
My second eldest sister named her son Muhammad.
As for my third sister, God has given her both Ahmed and
    Muhammad.'

The child smiled and said,
'I am Muhammad, my father is Muhammad, and my grandfather
    is Muhammad.
So I am Muhammad, son of Muhammad, son of Muhammad.'
I said, 'What could be nicer or better
Than someone called Muhammad.'
I love you, beloved Muhammad.
I love you! I love you! I love you,
And love all who love you,
Beloved Prophet of God.

The Failure of Ink Makes Me Sad

My morning and evening are spent in peace.
The afternoon brings amusement,
The evening embraces me,
And takes over my night,
And leaves me no more than a dead spirit.
But I never forget
To worship God.

I read and write,
And doze and wake up.
I feel happy at the writing of a pen;
The failure of the ink makes me sad.
But I never forget
To worship God.

I suffer and I complain
To close friends and to the general public;
A friendly ear captivates me;
The happiness of an enemy frightens me.
But I never forget
To worship God.

I see confused, lost people,
I love with the drunkards,
And I share the fun of those who are having a drink.
And I see haughtiness and the overbearing,
Suspicion and concern,
Faith,
And Certain Truth.
But I never forget
To worship God.

I go back to my castle,
I settle in my house,
Where my family and relatives live,

As well as my children and my wife.
I yearn for a warm meeting,
And aspire to a love I have been waiting for.
But I never forget
To worship God.

In my brotherly relations with friends,
In the sweet talk exchanged with loved ones,
I dive to the depths,
Looking for the secret, the deepest point
Of exchanged kindness and amity.
But I never forget
To worship God.

In-between these things,
Throughout these things,
My soul and my spirit feel at rest.
My heart beats in response
To the trustworthy, elect guide and teacher,
To the well-established love,
To deeply-rooted infatuation,
My spirit sings prayer, asking for blessings
Upon the Prophet of God,
Upon the one God loves,
Muhammad, son of Abdullah.
May God have His blessing upon him.
People pray for blessings for him,
The universe smiles at him.
I love him! I love him! I love him,
And love all who love him,
Beloved Prophet of God.

The Greatest Murdered Woman, the Martyr

Our world lives in wide-spreading darkness,
As if we were in the Stone Age.
In the morning we have a sick sun,
And in evening an eclipsed moon.
And dreams? Even dreams
Commit suicide while asleep.

But, when I explore the inner most of, and test,
My children,
The children of my homeland,
I am at the point of seeing
A newly-born dawn,
And I almost touch the new morning.
It is as if I see in front of me
Abubakr, Omer, and Ali,
And Al-Khansa, Naseebah, and Fatima.
I see modesty and reverence;
Friendliness and firmness;
Learning, noble birth, and piety.
And I see many millions
Represented by a few people.
I see tears, coming down like rain,
Carrying heavy burdens,
Washing sorrows,
Mobilizing men and bringing out their brave spirits.

I see Naseebah live
To achieve immortality, to be
The greatest murdered woman, the martyr.
I see Fatima, the daughter of the man I love,
Whose light spreads out
Through deserts, prairies, and seas,
Both near and far,

I see them veiled,
Content, and devoted in their worship.
I see my sons and the sons of my homeland
Preoccupied with God's worship
And with Jihad for their homeland and their faith.
They ask and ask again
'Where shall we die?
On what land shall we be martyred?
In the Philippines, Afghanistan, or Palestine?
Would martyrdom be our lot,
As it was for
Our early predecessors?
Will we unify the Muslim World?
Will nations of the earth fear us?
Will we regain for Islam
Its prominence and security?'

Both you and I answer,
'Yes, yes, and again yes.
Yes, we are God's soldiers.
Yes, we are the remainder of God's worshippers.
Yes we are the ones God has conscripted
To serve the nation of the Master of the creatures, Muhammad,
May the blessing and peace of God be upon him,
The beloved chosen man, Muhammad.'

You, for whom the universe trembled
Out of fear for you;
You, to the rhythm of whose footsteps
The earth danced,
We are glad and happy
That he is one of us, and we belong to him.
We love him! We love him! We love him!
And I love him! I love him! I love him,
And we love all who love him,
And I love all who love him,
Beloved Prophet of God.

While I Was Circumambulating the Ancient House

On a Monday,
I was circumambulating the House of God,
I was a guest of my master Ismail,
Grandfather of Adnan
And the Adnanites.

I remembered that I was one of the hybrid Arabs
And remembered some brothers of ours
In Yemen, land of the pure Arabs.
I remembered the throne of Solomon and Sheba.
I remembered the angels,
The jinn, and Satan.

I remembered my friend
In the Central Region,
Yes, I remembered Abdulrahaman,
And said to myself
That he does not look like a man from the Central Region.
It must be that one of our grandfathers
Emigrated from Honoured Makkah
To the Towbad Mountain,
And there, he must have married, perhaps more than once,
And must have fathered
Scores of sons
And scores of daughters.

And while I was circumambulating the Ancient House,
I remembered one
Of God's verses in the Quran:
'God and His Angels send blessing on the Prophet.'

Overwhelmed, awed, and submissive,
I prayed for God's Blessings

For the Prophet of the Creator,
The One-and-Only Creator, the Irresistible.

Let us all pray for blessings
For the illiterate, trustworthy, chosen man,
Offspring of Abraham and Ishmael;
For the man whose love refreshes one's heart,
And makes the sick recover.
I love him! I love him! I love him,
And love all who love him,
Beloved Prophet of God.

I Am the Virgin, a Bride of Those Who Fear God

In the same month as this,
Within the lifetime of the world,
The Quran was revealed to the Guide of humanity,
And has dawned over the whole universe
So disgrace committed suicide,
Dishonour removed itself,
Debauchery was vanquished,
And Satan was dumbfounded.

In the same month as this
Within the lifetime of this world,
Verses of the Book of Evidence
Poured into the ears of an orphan,
Who did neither read nor write.
He was taught by the One Who taught man
That which he was ignorant of.
He was disciplined by the Lord of
Distinction between right and wrong.
He was shaken by Gabriel, peace be upon him,
Who told him, 'Read!
In the name of thy Lord and Cherisher, Who created –
Created man, out of a mere clot.'
Muhammad knew with absolute certainty
That these were the words of God, the Real,
The Lord, the Deity.
Words which no falsehood can approach,
Absolute, conclusive words.
Were revealed to the pure and handsome
Muhammad, the virtuous and trustworthy.

In the same month as this
Within the lifetime of this world,
Arid deserts were watered,

Sleeping peoples were awakened,
Rational, wise people felt reassured,
Awkward, ignorant ones ridiculed,
And eternal paradise kept saying,
'I am the residence of believing Muslims.
I am a lofty mansion.
I am the shade for tormented repentants.
I am the spring for the thirsty hopeless.
I am a garden with blooming branches.
I am a matchless beauty.
I am the arts; I am the different colours.
I am the impossible wine.
I am happiness; I am reassurance
And I am the virgin, a bride of those who fear God.'

In the same month as this
Within the lifetime of this world,
Muhammad, the master of the people,
The most loved one of all people,
Fasted, abstaining from food and drink
For the sake of the Everlasting, the Self-Subsisting,
    All-Forgiving God.
He consoled widows and orphans,
Kept the secret of fallen women,
Urged people to cover up for sinners,
Brought close to his side
Those who sought forgiveness from God, who repented,
    who came back to the fold,
And gave all that he had to the poor and unfortunate.

O Muhammad, whom God loves,
O Muhammad, whom we all love,
Who is our intercessor on the Appointed Day –
We pray for God's blessings for you and we salute you.
And I love you! I love you! I love you,
And love all who love you,
Beloved Muhammad,
Prophet of God.

My Soul Found Comfort in the Presence of the Creator

One evening
That offered neither delight nor ecstacy,
There were no friends close by,
And gloom dominated the evening,
Filling it up with sorrow and restlessness.

Pleasure trembled in fear;
Intimacy ran away in dismay;
Delight trotted away in sorrow:
Gloomy ashes occupied
All areas
In my belief and my intuition
Reaching all the way to my heart.

I had friendly conversation with the tracks of departed
      loved ones,
With the roads of pain.
I told myself that I would say to every wretched person
Who stays up at night when loved ones are near or when
      they are far,
For the sake of love or hatred,
That he should know and make sure
What exactly he wished for.
Did he wish the happy feasts
Of enemies to bleed?
Did he wish the clouds of treachery to rain
Blood and wash all hearts
And extinguish the fires of hatred
Making them white and smooth.

I sobered up and told myself,
'Hatred is consuming my heart
And destroying my house and my being.

I must take refuge in God
And expel, from my soul and my heart
The devils of black hatred;
I must wash myself with white love.'

My soul found comfort in the presence of the Creator,
The Avenger, the All-Powerful, in Whose hands is the
    destiny of all souls.
My heart was refreshed
By praying for blessings for the Prophet of God.
I got up, performed the rite of ablution and prayed.
My heart was relieved,
My self was calm,
I thanked God,
And I joined God in blessing
His Prophet.
God gives him His blessing and salutes him,
I love him! I love him! I love him,
And love all who love him,
Beloved Prophet of God.

Beloved Prophet of God
(On the Birthday of the Beloved One, I Remembered This Story)

He maliciously said, smiling,
'Ali is going to marry Fatima.'
Some listeners, being ignorant, wondered,
And all men of learning, who knew, were puzzled.
As for the ignorant ones, they asked in surprise,
'How would he marry her,
When he is already her husband?'
While those who knew wore the robe of sorrowful exasperation.

Hypocrites were happy at what their malicious members said.
The news spread out,
As fire in a haystack,
While the people of Bright Madinah
Either knew or did not
Until the news was confirmed
To all people.

Ali wants to marry another Fatima,
Daughter of Abu Jahl.
How could Ali cause unhappiness to the Mother of the Two
    Lights,
Hassan and Hussein,
And she is the flourishing, blooming
Daughter of God's Prophet?
My father, mother and children would redeem your life with
    theirs!
Would that my blood
And the blood of my family
Be spilled if it could prevent a single iota of your anger,
Beloved daughter of a beloved man!
I love you! I love you! I love you,
And love all who love you,
Beloved Prophet of God.

111

Who can vex the Blooming Lady,
Daughter of the impeccable Khadijah,
The Queen of Arab Women,
The first one to believe in the Prophet of God,
She who wrapped him up
And warmed him
When he came to her from the Cave,
Trembling,
Repeating what the Angel Gabriel had told him,
'Read!
In the name of thy Lord and Cherisher, Who created –
Created man, out of a mere clot of congealed blood;
Proclaim! And your Lord is Most Bountiful,
He Who taught me the use of the pen,
Taught man that which he knew not!'
I love you! I love you! I love you,
And love all who love you,
Beloved Prophet of God.

Who has all the glories,
As well as noble birth and an illustrious family?
Who is known for hospitality and generosity,
Devotion and fidelity,
Patience and tolerance,
Forbearance and carefulness,
Perseverance and diligence?
None but her,
Blooming Fatima,
For her mother is Khadijah
And her father is God's Prophet.
She was born
While Makkah was busy
With the rebuilding of the Ka'ba.
In her childhood
The people of Makkah named her father
The Trustworthy,
And he settled the differences among Arabs
And placed the Black Stone
With his noble hands
In the absolutely secure spot.
When she was five,

Inspiration came
The God's Prophet.
I love you! I love you! I love you,
And love all who love you,
Beloved Prophet of God.

Days passed,
And the Prophet for all people emigrated
To the Good town of Madinah.
The chaste blooming virgin
Was now at the age of nineteen
And senior Companions proposed to her.
Among these the Honest One and the Arbiter
The Sincere and the Arbiter, asked for her hand
But the Prophet, Father of Ibrahim,
Gave them no answer;
He resorted to silence.
He left the matter
Up to the Kind Handler.
I love you! I love you! I love you,
And love all who love you,
Beloved Prophet of God.

But
How did Ali, son of Abu Talib, make his proposal of marriage
To the blooming daughter of Muhammad,
Daughter of Khadijah?
After he asked for her hand,
How did he marry her?
And what did the chosen man do
So as to marry her to
His cousin Ali,
The Imam of those who fear God?
I love you! I love you! I love you,
And love all who love you,
Beloved Prophet of God.

He smiled!
Muhammad rejoiced.
Birds sang.
Joy and happiness competed in jealousy.

Angels yielded
To God's command,
For it was at the command of God
That Fatima married Ali
I love you! I love you! I love you,
And love all who love you,
Beloved Prophet of God.

The beloved one asked
His future companion in paradise
What he had to offer
As dowry for Fatima?
The valorous, well-known fighter,
Owner of the vertebrated sword, replied,
'All I have is my mare, my armour, and my weapon;
And these are my equipage in Jihad.'
The Prophet, with his known submission
To the God of mankind, said to him,
'As for the mare, keep it for Jihad,
And as for the armour, sell it
And get me the price.'
So he sold it to Othman, the man-with-two-lights.
I love you! I love you! I love you,
And love all who love you,
Beloved Prophet of God.

So Ali married Fatima.
She was the first woman he married,
And did not marry another
As long as she lived.
Her wedding was attended
By senior companions,
Abubakr, Omer, Othman,
Al-Zubeir and Talha.
They all ate Medina dates.
I love you! I love you! I love you,
And love all who love you,
Beloved Prophet of God.

The dowry of Al-Zahra
Was four hundred and eighty Dirhams.

The man I love bought
For Ali and Fatima
A bed, a pillow,
The fur of a ram
(As a cover and a rug),
A stone handmill, a waterskin,
And two bracelets of silver.
I love you! I love you! I love you,
And love all who love you,
Beloved Prophet of God.

On the blessed night
The father of the bride
The Prophet who is a light to the world,
Went to the house of Ali,
And soon the house of Chaste Fatima.
He asked the maid,
'Is my brother here?'
Um Ayman smiled and said,
'Your brother? He is marrying your daughter!'
The Trustworthy man, as dear to me as my soul, said,
'Yes, he is my brother in this world and in the Hereafter.
God, I command her and her offspring
To your protection from the Evil and Rejected Satan.
God, let them have a lot of offspring,
And let their offspring be good.'
I love you! I love you! I love you,
And love all who love you,
Beloved Prophet of God.

The man I love
The house of the woman I love.
She looked at him with tears in her eyes.
He told her,
'Don't cry, Fatima,
I have given you in marriage to the most upright man
        in his faith,
And the best learned one.
And I gave you in marriage only
At God's command.
Didn't you know that

He is my brother in this world and in the Hereafter?'
I love you! I love you! I love you,
And love all who love you,
Beloved Prophet of God.

And the Blooming Lady begot
Two children whom Muhammad commended
To God's protection
Against the Evil and Rejected Satan.
They are the cream of young men who are destined for Paradise.
They are the dye and the henna,
The joy and delight,
The flame and light,
The two shining stars,
Hassan and Hussein,
Of whom the giver of light,
The bright moon,
The most Trustworthy man, said,
'O God, I love them,
So please love all who love them!'
I love you! I love you! I love you,
And love all who love you,
Beloved Prophet of God.

Fatima wanted
A maid
To help her
In house-keeping.
She asked her father
To look into this matter,
And Muhammad said to Fatima,
'Shall I tell you what is better than what you have come for?'
The obedient daughter replied,
'O yes, Prophet of God, do!'
Inspired by God, the Prophet said,
'It is words which Gabriel has taught me;
You praise God, thank Him and say,
"God is great,"
Thirty-three times
Following each prayer.'
I love you! I love you! I love you,

And love all who love you,
Beloved Prophet of God.

He became angry,
The tolerant man became angry,
The tolerant man became angry,
He who 'to Believers is most kind and merciful.'
He went up the rostrum and said,
'The clan of Hisham, son of Al-Mugheirah,
Have sought my permission to give their daughter
In marriage to Ali.
But I withhold my permission.
Yes, I do not permit.
Fatima is a part of me,
And what angers her angers me.'
Ali did not make Fatima angry, never,
As long as she lived.
I love you! I love you! I love you,
And love all who love you,
Beloved Prophet of God.

Aisha, Mother of Believers,
Said about Fatima,
'I have seen none of God's creatures
Who is more like the Prophet of God
In conversation and way of speaking
Than Fatima.'
I love you, grandmother of mine,
I love your beloved one,
And I love all who love him.
O beloved Prophet of God.

Muhammad was sick.
Yes, he, the Thankful, Chosen, Praiseworthy, Trustworthy
Leader of all Believers,
Was sick just as all human beings get sick
As they have done since the Creation,
And as they will do to the Day of Judgement.
Fatima was
At his bedside.
He told her something in private,

And she wept,
Then he told her something else, also in private,
And she laughed.
She did not want
To reveal the secret to any one.
But when he died, she told the secret:
'He said to me that he would die of that sickness,
And I wept,
Then he whispered to me that I would be the first member of
    his family to follow him,
And I laughed.'
I love you! I love you! I love you,
And love all who love you,
Beloved Prophet of God.

And the Blooming
Fatima,
The thankful, the worshipper, the God-fearing woman,
Died and was the first member of his
Family to follow him,
As he had told her, which was good news to her.
My master, my Lord,
Beloved one of men old and men of later times,
Master of all creatures and all messengers of God,
The man God loves.
I love you, Fatima,
I love your beloved one,
And I love all who love him,
Beloved Prophet of God.

PART SEVEN

Islam
and the
Arab Nation

Here I Come, My Lord, Here I Come

'Welcome, please feel at home!
Whom would you be?
Who are you?
Are you, brother, from Arabia?
From Hijaz, from Najd, from Yemen?
Or are you, brother, one of the Arabs of the North?
Are you from Egypt?
Or are you from Morocco?
No, No, you must be from Iraq?
You are, then, from one of the Gulf countries?
Or from the extreme south?
You must be, then?
From Oman, from Hadhramout,
Or from Aden?'

Like the pyramids, like the Sphinx,
He did not utter a word, He gave no answer
He stared at my face
Looked me boldly in the eyes,
Read my thoughts in depth,
Slipped into the depth of my soul,
And forced me to resume talking.

I said, 'I have reached a decision;
I am positive that you are from an Arab country.
You profess the religion of Arabs,
And you are one of the grandsons of
Those who had kindled the wick of freedom
In the usurped ignorant territories
And the oppressed, lost souls.'
He smiled and his face gleamed,
His sorrows disappeared and were no longer seen,
His frown and his scowl dissolved,
Upon his lips gathered
A host of pleasure expressions,

And his eyes were lit
With the light of happiness and faith.

Finally, he spoke. He said,
'I am from Honoured Makkah,
My grandfather immigrated to Madinah, the City of Light.
Originally I am from Yemen.
The offspring of that grandfather were born everywhere,
On high mountains,
Low plains, and sandy desert –
They were all giants who dared the impossible.
My clan's horses set their hoofs on lands of
The East and the West, the South and the North,
The lands of Persians, Romans, and all nations.
My folks turned the dream into reality,
And those who were thirsty at length quenched their thirst,
After frequent drought which plagued
My house, my relatives, and all tribes,
Thousands of times and for thousands of years.

'About one thousand and four hundred years ago,
The hoped-for Prophet,
Of the same origin and the same clan as mine,
Appeared with a Message that brought good
And caused satisfaction,
Engraving on the rocks of ignorance
Verses that actually spoke out
And carried the banners of Monotheism,
Verses which celebrated a feast of glory
And predicted through pictures and signs
That can only mean a Messenger was sent by God.

'In the bosoms of the drought nations slept;
They lived in the burning squalor of shameful deeds;
They trafficked in animals and human beings;
They exchanged conspiracy for murder;
They were prey for plagues of the ignorance;
They were buried by the earthquake of the injustice
In a grave haunted
By the submission, hunger, and the poverty of my clan.

'About one thousand and four hundred years ago,
My hopes rode a she-camel
And went all over Arabia,
Cleansing it of all the blemishes of the ignorance.
Thus, unique men emerged out of it,
And they disseminated the guiding light
And buried all delusions and all serfdom
Under the earth, in graves,
In all countries.

'About one thousand and four hundred years later,
Someone came along and spoke without modesty;
"You, people of Arabia," he said,
"Are rich by mere chance,
Through energy or petroleum."
The blind ignorant speaker has forgotten
That we, in Arabia,
Have given the world
Coffee, horses, and palm-trees.
We offered security and peace
From Makkah and Medina.
The Light of Islam emanated
Truly and insistently
From Arabia.

'In this time of our, the present time,
Life evolves and goes on
In Europe, in China,
In America, in Japan,
On land, in the sea, in the air,
On every land, and in every sky
Supplied out of the bowels of our earth, which are full
Of energy or petroleum,
And of an ambitious hope
For a new world, a clean world,
That cancels submission,
Heals wounds,
Orders hunger
To disappear and be extinct,
And mutters in reverence,
"Here am I, my Lord, here I come.

You have no partner, and here I come.
Praise, Grace and Supreme Power are all yours;
You have no partner,
And no one is wealthy but You.'

Idols are Smashed by our Hands

Right from the beginning,
They wanted to break Islam into pieces,
And up to the end,
They will fight the faithful throngs,
They will fight throngs who believe
In God, the One and Only,
The Supreme and Irresistible,
The Most Merciful.

We, the young,
Are God's soldiers,
The soldiers of Islam;
We fight the brigades of infidelity.
The world is small in our eyes,
And the Hereafter gets bigger and bigger in our hearts,
And idols are smashed by our hands.

I shall narrate to you,
Remind you of,
The events of history,
All satanic types,
And those who angered God,
And who are wayward and lost.

Two armies assembled in the Land of Peace;
An army fought,
And the other sang enthusiastically,
Pushing the greater devil on to victory.

The two armies took over
My land;
Al-Quds became
The capital of the tyranny.

The faithful throngs were mustered;
They fought and fought and won.
The dust of polytheism cleared up.
Falsehood turned coward when faced by Salahuddin.
And to the land of Faith
Al-Quds and all other cities were restored.

Following the victory, we were firmly certain
That we were a nation that can never be defeated, never be
    subdued.
Then there were days when we dominated,
Infidelity was defeated,
And the devil was vanquished.

With the passage of time,
Our minds and hearts, as well as
Limbs, slackened.
The devil slipped in,
Playing with perishable funds,
Using transient glory as a bait,
And feeding our carnal appetites.

Those who had invoked God's wrath
And those who went astray never forgot
Their subjugation, humiliation, and defeat
At the hands of Salahuddin's soldiers.
So, in their spiteful hearts a burning fire blazed,
Asking for the grandsons of Salahuddin's soldiers.

Enemies of righteousness made an alliance
That was signed by the devil.
We live today
The way we are:
We have forgotten, moved away from, and quarrelled with
    our religion.
And from the top of the mountain, we have thrown down
    our faith.

My people, I warn you
Of a black day,
A day that is darker than those that have passed,

A day on which you will win victory
Only through Islam
And true faith.

PART EIGHT

From the Depth
of My Heart I Say to
You

I Am to Be Blamed; I Am the Loser

Clouds of mist cover my coasts
My boats are at a loss, confused, cannot make out
The way to salvation, to certitude.
I go from port to port, searching for shelters.
No eye cares to look at me,
No roof covers me,
And torrents throw me to other torrents.

My dreams sink in the seas of despair.
My hopes die in the waters of misery.
In my prayers, I seek protection from the Most Merciful;
In my solicitations, I seek forgiveness from the Oft-Forgiving.
Yet, while I am deep in prayer,
The devil tempts me and thus abducts me.
He makes me forget my purpose and my quest.
He tempts me with mature wine,
With sleepy-eyed beauties,
And with the type of Godless evenings that I have already
        abandoned.
He makes me forget what I wanted and hoped for
In the form of mercy, pardon, and forgiveness,
And he diverts my attention from the prayer-rug with immoral
        thoughts.
He fills my prayer niche with ashes
And entices me away from hearing the Muezzin
Calling for the worship of God from a minaret.

I forget my solicitations and prayers;
I sober up for the night's drinking bout
And wake up from my sleep during the day:
I shout at the top of my voice, 'Murderer!'
I am the guilty one, the inadvertent one,
Who trails in the silk of sin.
And I am the lost one who has collapsed,
The collapsed one, in search for a lighthouse

That would guide me to a safe haven,
And in my nightmares and dreams,
I see Moguls and the Tartars,
While in my wakefulness when I am most sober,
I see my enemies, my tormentors.
My soul asks my mind,
'Who will commit suicide? who will be victorious?
The Arabs of tomorrow or the Jews of Israel?'

I am, right from the beginning and at the end,
Exhausted, crushed, seeking refuge;
I don't hear, I don't see, I don't know;
And my question-marks
Do not know the answer,
And are far away from the decision-making process.
I ask again and again,
'Shall I do injustice to the night?
Shall I find fault with the day?
Shall I spit on the world?'
No, No, No,
I ... I ... I ...
Am the defeated one;
I am the loser;
I am the one to be blamed.

Have You Caught Sluggishness Diseases?

She gently reproached me;
She spoke kindly, she asked tenderly,
'You forget my birthday?
You forget our wedding anniversary?
You forget the date of our first meeting?
You forget our first-born,
Our heir, our son?
You forget the youngest?
You forget the happiness?
You forget the holidays?
You go so far in forgetting as to forget
My staying up at night and my bowing in the
        worship of God?'

You think that I am not paying attention,
That I am asleep,
That I am unaware
Of your steps, your waiting,
Your fear, your concern,
Your quiet, your stillness,
Your confusion, and your halting.

I have been searching,
Asking for a reason?
I found out that I was not paying attention,
That I was asleep,
That I was unaware,
And that you have done the strangest thing,
The queerest and most astonishing thing.

They whispered in my ear, they said
You were infatuated with Zeinab!
Zeinab? My companion and friend?

They also said to me
You were madly in love with your Leila!
Every Leila from the time of being born
Carries the virus of deformed love and madness.
Haven't you read that Qays
God mad and turned into a symbol
Of alienation, loss, and reproof.

'My mate,
You who have shared my love and my anguish,
You who have shared romance and suffering,
You who have shared the question and the answer
Mate of the past days –
My friend;
Friend of my hours, days, and years;
Friend of my sleeplessness and my pillow,
Friend of my life –
Have you caught sluggishness diseases,
And have, therefore, forgotten the meeting and how
    close we are?
Have forgotten the days of tragedy?
Have forgotten the days of crises?
Have forgotten the clear and pleasant days?
And have forgotten – you used to make an assault
And capture my little heart.

'And I – I am the one that loves and has been enslaved by love.
You know well
How a smile makes me yield
And a frown prompts me to fight,
How I am as smooth and fine as silk
And as fierce as a harsh, overcast day.

'Beloved,
I shout at the top of my voice
That I am jealous, I am jealous;
I am crazy and I am foolish,
While you are grave and composed;
And I am an uproar, and you are quiet itself.

'Beloved
Keep away your legions of disaffection,
And put out, beloved, the hell of your absence.
Draw upon your lips
Honest smiles of satisfaction;
Draw upon your face
True sign of contentment and faithfulness.
And swear, I beg you to swear,
To make up with me and not to stay away.
Let us be as we used to,
Fighting pain, having fun with happy hours
And holding every night
A festival of songs
For love and life.'

My Mother Asks Every Traveller

I dream! How often do I dream?
And what do I dream of?
I dream of falling asleep
On my mother's chest.
I dream of sitting
On my father's lap.
I dream of going back
To my grandfather's land.
I dream of meeting my end
On the soil of my homeland.

Will my dream come true
In my own time?
Am I destined to return?
Or is my destiny to abandon the homelands?
I am sure I will not hesitate
To go back,
But I walk like a captive
Who has been arrested by the devil.

My mother asks every traveller
And urges him, saying,
'My son, look for my son.
He is brown like you,
An Arab giant,
Good-hearted like you,
Handsome and shy,
And generous like you.'
My father shouts at sleeping people
And whispers to those awake.
He solicits and begs.
He says with emphasis,
'I am looking for my son.

'I left him when his silvery fancy headband

Was like the sun on foreheads.
His quilt was like moonlight
On dark nights, in the utter darkness.
His hands were like a thunderbolt,
Like the collision of clouds with clouds.
His eyes were those of a hawk
Turned free.

'My son, who is happy
With grass and green branches –
My son, who is infatuated with
Narrow blue eyes –
My son, who is madly in love
With red and blond colours –
My son, who is wallowing
In the mud of yellow freedom –
My son, who hates a vast, innocent desert,
And high, lofty mountains –
My son, who has left behind
Wide, black eyes –
My son, who is lost away
From a chaste, brown beauty –
My son, it is you who is rejected;
It is you who is metamorphosed, you who are an ape;
It is you who is the laughing-stock of enemies.
My clamorous son
Inside the Unforeseen,
I know, and your mother knows,
Your homeland knows
That we miss you.
Why, then, my son,
Do you shun your folks
And abandon your homeland?'

Lamis Is Like Satan

My land, my waters, my bed,
My house, my homeland, and my honour
Are in the regional market
Are in the international market
On auction, for sale.

This homeland, at this time of ours
Is desecrate, defiled in the open,
And I am the broker, the promoter, who cries,
'This is my land and these are my waters;
A beautiful nymph from paradise is asleep on my bed.
Everything is there before your eyes,
Clear and in the open.
Who bids?

'Pay attention and choose well!
Be careful, as I make no distinction!
Choose well, as I don't differentiate between
The clever and greedy
And sincere relatives,
Or the innocent,
And I publicly declare that
This soil, this homeland
Is for sale or rent
To whoever pays a high price.'

Mayyaddah twists and sways,
Lamis is like Satan,
And Ghaddah throws herself
Onto the lap of vice and of slaves,
Sells her cover and veil,
Rents her bed and pillow,
And shamelessly demands
Higher rent from the tenant.

138

As for me,
I turn my face away in disdain and shout,
'Welcome, all comers!
May the pockets of tourists be full!
There is no difference between laughing people
And frowning indignant ones.
All I am interested in
Is romance and the whims of the frivolous.

'Wake up and be careful!
For I am very clever, I am a person of sound judgement;
I know how to make my hit,
And I know how to fill my pocket
And build my paradise with unlawful funds.

'Woe to me, what a shame!
I have built my high buildings
On soft sand
And thought that I would have a rest,
That I am now immortal
In the world of suffering, in the mortal world,
That I was one of the rich,
One of the very richest.

'And now that it is the right time,
Now that it is too late,
I keep telling and saying
To relatives, neighbours and strangers,
"Once upon a time,
There was a beautiful, a friendly homeland,
A homeland which the seas used to flirt with
And gardens lived in the neighbourhood."

'Now when it is too late,
I blame every body.
The reason? What will the reason be?
Are pockets now empty of money?
Or perhaps they have conspired:
A leader in Alaska
Or a leader living in the South Pole?
Or have the Big Powers

Discovered that there are treasures inside me?
And that there are bridges over my land
Connecting the thirsty and the greedy
With the valleys of gold.

'What can I say? What can I add?
When those who are sitting on decayed limbs
On the homeland, on the parts,
Are imagining and made drunk by their imagination,
Which urges them to commit crimes.
They fight, they wrestle, and they look
For a dictionary, a book,
That would decipher all enigmas.

'In the end, the last thing to be said is:
He who buys the world,
Sells the hereafter.
He who buys wealth
Sells the land and the waters
And the bed, the seas,
And the homeland.'

PART NINE

Ideas
and
Meditations

I Have Lost My Vessels on Sea Routes

The language of conversation is out of order.
I drafted on my books and papers
Words of passionate love.
I inscribed on stone the language of courting
And wooing.
I made expressions of love
Common to all lovers.
I sought assistance from Anter Ibn Shaddad,
And begged Qays and Jamil for help.
And I solicited aid
From all poets.

I implored Ibn Abi Rabee'a,
The poet with the big heart.
I kissed the head of the Poet Laureate,
The Prince of Poets.
I travelled to the land of the pyramids
From Aswan to Cairo,
From clarity to ambiguity.
I sailed with my vessels
In the basin of the Nile River,
Looking for the throne of love.

I inquired about the lost,
I shouted at the patient,
I wrote to the ambitions,
I inquired, I shouted, and I wrote.
There was no echo, no answer, and no response.

I lost my vessels on sea routes.
Hearts were sorry for my toil.
I asked for people who would understand my expressions,
And I felt sad at the sorrow in my words.

My love passion has dropped down and was scattered;
Poetry and poets toyed with it.
I was determined to find an answer;
The answer and response was,
'You are the stranger, the intruder.
You are a little amount, and we are a lot.'

Here I come back to you, I beg you
To protect me, to do me justice.
I ask again and again and again
Who is accusing them? Who is putting them on trial?
Who are surrounding them? Who are incriminating them?
Who is making the earth sink under their feet?
He dares and ventures,
And he calls me to climb and to sit
On the throne of love passion,
He informs them that I am noble,
Not a stranger,
Not an intruder,
And not a commoner.

After making some studies, I came to know
That all of them, every single one,
Are ambitious, aspiring to
The throne of love passion;
That Qays had described me
As an accursed devil;
Even Ibn Abi Rabee'a
Had asked and wondered,
'Who is he, that person?'
Who keeps up and competes with me
In love talk;
And the expressions of passion;
As for Al-Mutanabbi, he had said,
With self-esteem, loftiness, and haughtiness,
'I am the pioneer, I am the erudite,
And I am the elucidator who said,
"Horses, the night, and the desert know me
And so do the sword, the spear, and paper and pen."
So I am the leader, and I am the flag bearer.

Therefore, it is a crime, for you,
And an act of treachery, on my part, to think
Of love, mad, passionate love.'
From far, from a most remote spot,
The poet Ilya Abu Madhi announced,
'I am neither the culprit nor the lawyer,
Neither the bailiff nor the judge.
All I want is
To sit on the throne of love passion.'

At the beginning,
In the middle,
Or at the end,
My passion, my love, my mad, passionate love,
My ink and papers,
And my letters and lines
Are always a most wonderful conclusion.

May the Events of History All Perish

I shall re-write the history of mankind.
I shall make its heroes
Ordinary people,
And I shall turn the courageous into cowards.
As for rats –
By the way,
I love rats, I just adore them,
So why not have a rat ride
A wolf, direct it, and lead it;
Tame it and turn it into a cat
That jumps from lap to lap.

From history books, we learn
That Brutus
Assassinated Caesar.
What nonsense is this?
It was Caesar who assassinated himself.

The history of lovers says
That Qays fell in love with Leila
And was mad just thinking of her.
This is forgery,
For Leila was the worst enemy,
And Qays could only be described
As a cheat.
As for that black Anterah,
He was the leader of the incompetent,
A hero of dissimulation;
His battles were all fought
In boudoirs.

May the events of history all perish;
My weapons will translate white, and black,
Red, blue, and yellow,
And all other colours.

They shall sweep the trees in a storm,
And they shall cause the corners of mountains to tremble.

You speak, and I shall speak.
Mention your names,
And I shall turn every truth inside out;
What I shall reveal is not what I conceal,
For I love to re-write human history
By turning it upside down and in reverse.

Don't be disturbed
For I, this person who is me,
Have changed the truths about myself,
And I am proud
That I am fair:
I have dealt with history
The same way I have dealt
And I deal
With myself.

I Beg You, Pay Attention and Be Alert

I imagine that I am on Mars,
On the highest mountain of Mars,
Surrounded by seven valleys.
The valleys become numerous,
Then I discover that I am surrounded at the twenty-first.
I snatch out my field glasses and scrutinize the scene.
I see clearly, very clearly,
A barbarious and fierce attack,
Meanly besieging, the turning
Around, the twenty-first.
And I say to myself, over and over,
"I am the one besieged at the twenty-first;
She conspires against me, she wants me,
Paying no attention to her own destruction,
Not knowing that her gown
Has been torn by surrounding hurricanes.
Now they are naked before the enemy.

Stupid am I; I only think
With the mentality of the Sultan.
Blind am I; I only see
With the eye of the Sultan.
Dumb am I; I only speak
With the tongue of the Sultan.
Deaf am I; I only hear
With the ears of the Sultan.
Senseless am I; I only feel
The fire of the Sultan.
Dull and indolent am I,
I only feel the sting of the Sultan's needles.
Illiterate and ignorant am I;
They only read to me
The views of the Sultan
That are written with the Sultan's ink.
Degraded am I; I could only rise

With a promotion from the Sultan.
Poor am I; I only got rich
With funds looted by the Sultan
Out of my subdual, my humiliation, and his tyranny;
Out of my hard life and deprivation;
Out of my sufferings in seas of blood
And destruction in the fire extinction;
And out of the mad rush of nations, in a league, upon me,
The same way that diners rush madly upon a pot,
As if I were a new and delicious dish,
A beautiful, full maiden,
Whom they want to be delicious and plan to have her raped.

You are not fighting me,
You are fighting yourselves,
And you will not kill me,
You will kill yourselves,
Without me you are out in the open,
Without me you will not reach the summit.
I am your supplies and equipage,
And you are nothing without me.

I beg you, listen to me, and comprehend what I say:
For you, to stand on the summit
And take lodging at the top
Will not be, will not take place.
It will only come to be and become legitimate
When I am with you,
When your idols are destroyed,
And when your dreams are cancelled.
They are idols you want me to worship,
And dreams which you want to shed my tears and my blood,
You give orders and conspire in order to fulfill.

Your flags are disfigured, imported;
Your language is cartoonish, confused;
Your clothes poorly fit you;
Your society is fed up with you;
And we, the closest to you, your neighbourers,
Look at you as strangers.
After all, you are like monkeys, like apes.

No, you will never, never be
Exactly and completely like them.

No, this matter will not take place,
No, nor will it be achieved or become legitimate,
Except by a revolution against imitation,
The ape's imitation of man;
Except by a rebellion against coercion,
Against acceptance of loss and humiliation,
And submission to a culture a civilization
That eats up man's soul,
And turns it into a cogwheel, a machine,
Which can only stop
At flaming gates,
Which draw them in and get them
Into the hell of fire.

You Who are Strangled with Silk

You, valley!
Valley with no echo!
You who seeks protection
From gardens with no dew!

You who are hungry,
Hungry and sitting at a table,
Without any drink or food!

You who wish for
Rain
Without clouds, without any clouds!

You who appeal for help
For the help of confusion,
Of intensive heat, of fire!

You who dream
Of a light-house!
In a bottomless
Blue sea!
You who are asleep
In bed,
Who are strangled with silk!

You who are awake,
Awake and enlightened,
You short-lived happiness.
You who are inadvertent,
Inadvertent and asleep, thus unaware
Of a great event which is taking place!

You who hate,
The world,
Life, and survival!

You who love,
A dear one,
But enjoy no closeness and no felicity!

You madman,
Mad with shameless dissipation,
My tears never dry up,
And my voice resounds like a wail!

You who are on your way,
From the very beginning
To your death with no price!

You who walk
Along a road
Without signs,
Without an end!

You who are subdued
Since your birth
By an old, new thing that you cannot see!

O you who are humiliated,
Resist
The soldiers of tyrants.

You fools
Who are in the streets,
In universities, at schools,
In companies, in shops,
On land, at sea,
And on every border,
You are in every land;
You are small,
And you are nothing, just nothing.

I am at a loss,
Where is the beginning?
Where is the end?
Where is the alternative?

No bottom, no big ones, no small ones,
No beginning, no end, no alternative,
No food, no silk,
No fire, no ashes,
No felicity, no clouds, no dew,
And no echo.

Would a Night and a Day Be Equal?

She said, 'You are old,
Like a few drops of water left in the bottom of a mug.
Your few hair have turned grey,
And you have shaved your beard,
To hide the passage of days,
And conceal the march of years.'

White cheeks that have
Blushed spilling happiness
From a rosy face, yours – asked,
'Have you dyed your eyebrows?
Have you lined your eyes
And your eyelashes?
And on your head, have you
Put a wig?'

I said, 'My hair has turned white;
I am satisfied with my white hair.
Would a night and a day be equal?
As for my wearing
A black wig
Dying my eyebrows,
And lining my eyes
And eyelashes,
I only do so
So that your two black eyes
May find a black mate.

'Do you know
That because of your figure
Nations were lost,
And for the sake of your two eyes
A war was started
And peace was lost.

'Are you aware of the significance of this?
Because of your extreme beauty,
A day got jealous,
The darkness of night turned white,
A desert narrowed,
And trees and flowers
Began to grow out in oases.'

My love that is hungry
To the desires of a maiden!
My day that complains of indigestion
Of too much magnanimity and wealth, and too many hopes!
My night that is empty of
A maiden love!
My hopes which are so far
From being near to maiden,
Who would look into my eyes,
Inflame my night,
And turn me back, with a glance,
Scores of years,
And I am once again at the prime of youth;
I become able in a moment
To extinguish the fire of love,
With a look, with a whisper
And with a meeting that would erase from my life
The helplessness of days.

Bring to the Killer the Tidings That He Will Be Killed

Arabic, you are unfortunate.
You, a forgotten word,
A faded sentence,
The victim itself,
Were raped in the darkness of the night
By an adulterer,
And stripped naked in the light of the morning
By a fornicator.
He brazenly talked
And impudently claimed
That you begot Arab nationalism.

How could a stranger beget
A relative?
How could an enemy rescue
A drowning man?
How could he liberate Palestine
While his fruits are atheist
His children are illegitimate,
His waters are mixed with mud,
His bread is kneaded with bitterness,
His tongue is dipped in meanness,
His voice is cold,
His words are rotten,
His waterskin is pierced,
His cups are cracked
His utensils are broken,
His sword is dripping blood,
And he recognizes no religion.

My folks, my people, my nation,
You wise men of my clan,
Intelligent men of my people,

Elite of my nation
Who wants security?
Who disapproves tyranny?
Who opposes coercion?
Who fights infidelity?
Who removes the ashes?
Who kills corruption?
Who develops the country?
Who rescues the victim?
Who shouts for freedom?
Who will board with me
The ship of salvation?
Who will sail with me
Into the great sea of peace?
Who will pay money
For the defeat of darkness?
Who will sacrifice his children?
Who will give his soul and body for the redemption of
The Muslim nation,
Muhammad's nation?

You who have promoted false doctrines
Among waves of guileless people and slaves;
You who have shocked by your scheming.
All who are close and all who are far
You have drunk the blood of the free,
You have watered the deserts,
You have poured into the seas
The blood of the noble brothers
Out of the artery and the vein.

You – it is you who have done this
You – it is you who are the killer,
You – it is you who have strangled
An embryo in the womb!
Bring to the killer the tidings
That he will be killed
Sooner or later.

PART TEN

Sorrows
and
Sad Thoughts

My Buried Sadness,
My Old Sorrow,
Speech Which is Free

The whisper of the moon
Is enough to intoxicate seas,
Captivate beauties, extremely beautiful women
Move the tender emotions of flowers,
Make the coast and the river dance,
Reveal the depth of passion, clearly,
As well as despair and frustration.
The waves of love go to sleep
In its eyes.
Between the eyelids, they come to a rest.
And on its eyelashes
Dreams sleep,
Seeking endearment and passion,
Looking for flirtation,
Handing over the reins and the bridle
To a smile, to sweet talk,
And delightedly, excitedly, singing
To the night, the long night,
And to the eyes, the fair eyes.

And oh for my buried sadness,
My old sorrow,
Speech which is free,
My sand, my soil, my dust,
My books, my notes and my papers!
How I yearned, worried about, and reproached later
Days which never came
And hours that did not like the idea of having me
Shape them and write them,
And did not want to surrender, submit, and confess,
So they dozed out in the streets of remote cities,
Slept on the roads of the forgetfulness,

161

Were awakened in the midst of glowing fire,
Were swallowed up by frozen squares,
And were swept away by a cold wind,
After some wayward sleeplessness,
That blasted my quiet and my calm,
After a madness that destroyed
My pen, my expressions, and my rhetoric.

My buried sadness,
My old sorrow,
Speech which is free,
I call you and I beseech you, asking,
'Where are my past days?
How can I possibly recognize
My future days?
Why has no one remembered
My past, sad days?
Why has no one warned me
Against oppressive future days,
Which flee in the silence,
Are overburdened with suffering,
Are drowned in the quiet,
And call my past days,
Pleading with them to come back to me,
My sad, perished days;
Entreating and begging them,
Kindly not to lead my tomorrow
To a new misery,
A stubborn misery,
A misery loaded with tragedies
And capable of celebrating nothing but boredom.

My old sadness
My buried sorrow,
Speech which is free,
I want to wake up!
I don't want to sleep!
I want a day like the sun,
A night like the moon,
An afternoon like pure light,
An evening like an agate stone.

I want minutes that run,
Hours that pass,
And days that close, with me
Like a newly-born child who has
Spent centuries and milleniums
Without being acquainted with the language of sleeplessness,
Without looking for anxiety,
Without learning the language of misery,
Without excavating for the roots of separation,
Without discovering that life is
A beginning and an end;
Union and disunion;
Defeat, grief, and collapse;
Without discovering that existence, or life,
Is a pulsation that speeds up and slows down,
Devours days,
Swallows years,
And consumes epochs;
That it is a mirage that blasts the void.

My buried sadness,
My old sorrow,
Speech which is free,
My moans sound without resonance,
They are lost in the vacuum,
And my sighs are answered by the state of loss.
As if they were groans without an echo,
Amity without a mate,
Arrogance without tolerance,
Meeting without handshakes,
Faithfulness without a friend,
Flirtation without emotion,
Being near without being in agreement,
Stubbornness without arrogance,
Usurping power without tyranny,
Intimacy without tenderness
Devotion to the desperateness of despair,
Or a ship that has broken down and sank
To the depths of an ocean.

Nobody Knows the Secret of My Eyes

My papers are turning yellow,
In my memory numbers are getting mixed,
And so do passing events
That took place years ago,
And my heart, O my heart,
Does not fall in love without assistance.

I used to walk on it,
Striking the earth with two;
Now that my bones are feeble,
I crawl with three,
My two legs and my staff;
I can only walk with three.

Nobody knows the secret of my eyes,
The secret of the joy, the secret of the scare,
And the secret of link between the heart and the eye cavity.

How severe are my trembling, coming days!
How sweet were my astonished, past days!
Was it my yellowish papers,
My blank memory,
And my falling in love?
No, it was my plight from the number of the lovers!

My tears have dried up.
My eyes have turned into valleys
In a sterile desert
With which rain has quarrelled,
And at which rain-clouds got angry,
While some furious storms
Killed dreams, hopes, expectancies.

I Breathe Through My Head

My pen has stopped to express
My misgiving, my anxiety;
My imagination has breathed its last;
And my letters and words have died.

I am swimming in smooth, moving sand;
I am diving, not to return,
In a dead sea;
I am running a race
Against still winds;
From a dead sea,
I am begging for live and new meanings;
And I am talking to a still mountain
That does not breathe.

No beating heart
Rescues my pens.
No love pushes me forward,
And refreshes my hopes.
Even my own destiny
Fails to foretell for me what is to come.

My books?
Words have vanished from the lines!
My ships?
Sailing has exhausted them and broken them up!
My sword?
It is asleep, and never comes out of its scabbard!
Even my perfume
Has been paralysed by despair!

I breathe through my head!
I see through my back!
I hear through my eyes!
I talk through my ear!

I feel my way
By my chest!
I read upside down!
With a broken pen do I write!
What a strange creature I am,
At whom other creatures wonder.

I Am Drowning in Despair

I was sad, going, through my tears,
Over all sad events.
I was broken-hearted, remembering
The blows I received from my days.
I was a prisoner of my sighs and pain.

My yesterday! My present day! My tomorrow!
My yesterday that is mixed with bitterness;
My present day that stands erect like a mountain,
Unwilling to budge or move;
My tomorrow that is on the alert,
Lying in wait for me to make a false move.

I am drowning in despair,
Surrounded on all sides
By black water,
Which is still like the water at the bottom of an ocean.

Am I a prisoner of melancholy?
Am I in the hold of a delusion?
Am I infatuated by the suspicions?
Or am I mad over darknesses?

I Overflow with Sorrow

The passion of love seizes me at the darkest hours of night,
So violently that hearts are shaken by my love
Souls collapse because of my regrets,
I overflow with sorrow,
And melancholy, full to the brim
With all sorts of agony, gets refreshed.

Not a single moment of happiness remains
That has not been wiped out by the swords of your glance
Whether in my waking hours or during my slumber.
No memory of our meetings is left
That has not vanished
In your jealousy or your quarrel.

My conqueror who has forsaken me,
Owner of that heart that is infatuated with you,
You, whose disaffection has dried up my pens
And made me speechless.

In the bitterness of your love,
Sugar refuses to dissolve;
The symbols of your disaffection
Spread out in all directions;
Passionate love has committed suicide;
The singing sparrow has divorced its love,
And the curtain falls
On the tragedy while it dances breathlessly.

I Know I Am in a Labyrinth

You, who have bewitched me and forsaken me:
My tears have not dried up,
My sadness has not slept,
My moans are friends
With loss and non-existence,
My burns, my wounds, and my ulcers
Are not cured and have not healed.
In despair I try to change my lot,
And in distress I try to resist my death.
I know I am in a labyrinth
And have lost my will;
I know that, you are the absolute master,
The chief, the headquarters;
And I know that you know
I am fighting my battle
With arms, provisions, and equipment
Whose secrets you are aware of and whose details you
　　　well know.

You, who have bewitched me and forsaken me,
Be generous, be gracious,
Be sympathetic as you used to be.
Find out, be just, and be sure of
My love, affection, and tenderness,
For my standing with your soldiers,
My wars against your disaffection,
My determination to be near you,
My submission for the sake of your forgiveness,
And my taking your side without your knowing it –
All of these, all the things I have mentioned,
Are because I am infatuated by your love,
Have surrendered to your charm;
Are because I have lost my will;
I cannot stand your desertion;
Are because I love you!

There Is No Light Without Fire

My pain,
My flagrant pain!
It plugs the ears of my joys,
Plants pain in my chest,
Calls my disasters,
Shakes my calmness,
Rocks my quiet,
Ridicules my bliss,
Leaves me a captive of anxiety,
Throws me to the pit of the end,
And drowns me in the well of nonexistence.

My pain,
My hypocritical pain!
It draws my sorrows
Into the flames of ardent love and passion
So my dreams
Are cooked in the ovens of agony,
Are served by devils,
Eaten by jinn,
And detested by angels.

My pain!
My genuine pain!
It shocks me with the truth
That says to me,
'There is no light without fire;
There is no joy without pain;
There is no sweetness without bitterness;
And happiness has no taste
Without conflict.'

I Feel Bored, Distressed and Gloomy

My heart has contracted,
My sweet days have disappeared,
I have forgotten what freedom is,
And states in which I was the master,
The eagle,
The leader advocating freedom,
Exist no more.

I am bored with flying and soaring,
I am fed up with freedom,
And I am determined to put on handcuffs.
I have tied myself,
Chained my heart,
Struggled so that my wealth
May grow, may vastly increase,
And fought so that my prestige
May become greater and greater.

I am now rich,
I have prestige,
People respect me,
But, I do not enjoy
My assets, prestige, and the respect of people.

I feel distressed and gloomy!
My dreams have crashed down from the summit
With the acquisition of assets,
The joys of freedom have escaped,
With the prestige I have achieved,
And all forms of happiness have run away
With the respect people show me.

What can be done with an unfortunate man,

Who has been made wretched by his wealth,
Tormented by his prestige,
And whose joys have killed themselves with the respect he has.

I secretly hear
Shouts calling for my downfall.
I have learnt and made sure that
All people are unanimous in believing I am a simple, naive
        person,
Who is overjoyed at the words of hypocrites,
Soars high above the world of reality
By fake, deceptive, dissembling
Voices and cheers,
Which cry loudly, 'Long live he, long live he!'

Quietly, it withers,
With a hushed up, silenced clamour,
With fear from my fits
Of rabid, mad fury.
They have frequently repeated for me to hear
A song – how fast it goes! –
A sarcasting song which says,
Long live he! Long live he! Long live he!

How terrible!
Distress eats me up,
I breathe boredom,
And my very life is full of gloom.
What miserable a creature I am
Ridiculed by all creatures.

As If We Were on the Day of Judgement

My rivers have dried up
My flood streams and my brooks have gone dry.
Is there a counselor?
Is there a guide?
Is there an aid?

Images are torn up in my imagination,
My situation gets slapped by inability,
My pens are heavily burdened by hesitation,
My ink revolts, digging up for the impossible,
My thoughts get tired and look for a rebellion,
My paper wails
And run eagerly after letters,
They cry for sentences
That they may write, may keep from sleeping,
May draft, may use to list down
The nights of sleeplessness,
The days of fear,
The years of the drought;
That they may cause to be disturbed and suffer,
Like a lover counting the hours of separation.

My reality that is filled with passion,
My reality that is immersed in remoteness,
Fallen prey to the hours of restlessness,
Consumed by cracks and by headaches,
Paralysed by a huge assembly of vacuum,
Humiliated by a bleak valley,
Which has lost its echo;
It does not repeat what it says –
My reality whose hopes met their end at the hand
Of a nest fallen to ruin.

Waves of sand
Have crawled into the oases,

Palm trees have dried up and all other trees have turned black,
And the springs of affection have receded,
And light has gone out while it is still daytime.
No inhaling, no exhaling, and no frog croaking;
The donkey has died, and there is no braying;
Tame cats
Are roaring like lions
That are searching for food;
Domestic dogs
Have abandoned their barking and loyalty.

Is there a counselor?
Is there a guide?
Is there an aid?
Everybody is preoccupied with himself,
As if we were on the Day of Judgement.

PART ELEVEN

Human Types

He Performs Prayers in Dissimulation and Dances Reverently

There are, deep in the supernatural world,
In the darknesses of the Unknown,
Turbulent tides of events which keep me sleepless,
Amaze me and I feel awed,
Push me and I feel awed,
Push me to submission and defeat;
There are horrible faces that scare me,
Whips that set my nights and days on fire,
Eyes that penetrate into my soul,
Looks that provoke my conscience,
Urge it, push it, order it
To wake up, sober up, get up,
To say what I am afraid of saying,
And not to hesitate in confirming
What I thought was absolutely impossible.

I see you in disagreement with one another.
It pains me to see you fighting one another.
I see how in clear daylight,
At the prime time of day,
Young, grown-up, and old men
Being slaughtered, assassinated, and dragged on the ground
Without any cause or reason.
I see him among you;
I see him eat and drink with you;
Frown, laugh, and cry;
Cool down, lose temper, and act;
Perform prayers in dissimulation, dance reverently;
Slyly sing God's praises;
Drink to the last drop;
Get drunk till he is fully intoxicated;
Enjoy only the music of hypocrisy
The day disturbs him, darkness makes him happy,

The truth makes him sick, agreement scares him,
He sleeps and wakes up to the sound of lies,
And he steals, cheats, and kills.

I tell you with absolute frankness,
And I testify
That I see him among you;
I see him, I can touch him,
I confidently see him among you –
I see the fictitious Messiah,
The impostor Messiah among you,
Igniting the fire of discord among you.

The Third Communiqué

My brain listened to the radio,
My eyes watched on television,
The announcement of a first proclamation, which said,
'Violence has taken over the power.'
Then, an inflated, hollow cat
Appeared on television.
I heard his voice with my own ears.
I saw his face with my two eyes.
I was shocked when he said,
'I am from you, to you, and for you.'

The following day, the same cracked voice
Rattled on the radio
And that inflated cat,
Appeared on the little screen,
Saying, with a frown and in an aggressive manner,
'We shall take over the money
For the sake of this people.'

It breaks my heart to witness the loss of this people,
To see hands that know only slapping,
Know only looting,
And that will burn the legacy of ancestors,
Will use the entire people as guinea pigs
In experiments stamped with the seal of atheism
Imported from abroad,
Aiming at burning with fire
All God's people.

Violence swaggers,
Looking haughtily and arrogantly;
Screaming, roaring, and shouting;
Thinking that we are mute,
That everybody is deaf and dumb,
That we are a cattle nation.

It goes too far in giving utterance
To all sorts of lies and deception.
A crazy man who has lost his mental balance
Plays the drums, pipes, and dances.

I thought I had prepared the right blow
For the communiqués of lies,
That I might be able to
Take a cover off,
Expose of an act of deception,
But nobody gave me the chance
To discuss communiqués
Which by now are two.
The first one was a lie,
And the second one was deception,
And while I was on a vortex
Of lies and deception,
A third communiqué was announced.
It declared that the country and the people,
The whole country and the entire people
Are, as of today,
Property of the inflated cat.
What can one say?
There is no might and power unless granted by God.

He Torments the Maidenhood of Maidens

He is a captive whose release is impossible,
A prisoner against whom the walls of his prison
     close tightly.
His day has turned into night;
The door of his night has been closed;
He thinks of love and of his beloved one;
He forgets, or pretends to forget;
He lives on the nonsense of his dreams.

His dreams reject reality,
Do not know what acceptance is,
And are not, at any rate, to be fulfilled.
His love has put on the cloak of desertion,
And escaped to a distant land.
His beloved has turned into mud,
That has dissolved in unholy water.

He offered himself for sale;
He was bought by Torment,
Loss bargained over his price
And planted him in a retired land,
Evil harvested him,
Tyranny grinded him,
Some jinn cooked him,
He was well cooked in the devil's pot.

He became a monitor
For hatred and obscenity;
He became chairman of
Rancour, incrimination, and impudence;
And he became chief of
Vice and meanness.

He longs for destructive storms;
He conspires to blast reunion,
And he insists on killing affection.

He rests in a city
In which fires have been burning.
He passes the evening chatting with skulls
And human skeletons.
He kills the childhood of children
And torments the maidenhood of maidens.
He ridicules an old man, advanced in years
And laughs at a forgotten widow.
Poor, poor is this person!
He has become a slave for the devil.

You Command and He Obeys

The traitor draws you to the snare with the honey of his deceit,
With his zeal, with the intensity of the false love,
With his bitter loyalty;
You command and he obeys;
He says, 'Whatever you command; whatever you want.'

You order to have the colour of white dawn
Turn into black eyeliner,
And he obeys.
You order that a free woman should beget a slave,
And he obeys.
You want the bee all tied up,
You want the hands of the ant tied to its back,
And he obeys.
He will obey your orders
Even though these were
Yawns to stop air.

How can he stop breezes?
Cut whispers?
Or to control
The wakefulness and sleep of insects?
Control sorrows and make them beget decorations?
Subjugate a free maid who is a sealed virgin.
The falsehood of treachery,
Or to the lowest deceptions.
How can he make the sun rise
From the west?!
Or make the ever-moving moon set
In the east?!

Whatever you order, whatever you want,
You order and he obeys.
This is the habit of a dishonest man.
He divorces

Lofty standards of moral values,
So that he may rule,
May become arrogant,
May become a lion or a tiger.
This is the habit of a dishonest man
Everywhere and at all hours:
Falsehood, deception, hypocricy
Frustrations, and wounds.

After unawareness,
After consciousness,
After sorrow,
And after it is too late,
You come to know and make sure
That bitterness is sweeter than the colocynth.

I Am a Poet Who Uses no Rhymes

They said, 'Who are you?'
They said, 'How and where from did you come?'
Some said,
'You are the shadow of illusion.'
Some of these said,
'No, in fact, you are anxiety itself
And you are a friend of distress.'
All of them said,
'You are the one nearby;
You are close to the poetry of prose.'

I said, 'I am outstanding,
A poet who uses no rhymes.
I am the poet whose hillock summits
Could not be reached by verse meters,
Green and beautiful hillocks they are,
That were irrigated with my free letters
They were refreshed; they turned green then red.
Some flowers in a valley turned yellowish.

'No words with a greater ability than mine
Have ever been known.
No perfume of a better quality than mine,
Was ever smelled.'

They said, 'You, you are a conceited man
No, in fact, you are a mad one.'
They said a malicious thing,
Determined to harmonize
With a pen that does not recognize any poetry or prose,
That does not have any rhythm.
You are, then, an agent
Of an investigation or intelligence bureau;
You are an enemy of Palestine;
And draft pages

Begging for sorrow,
Mobilizing the soldiers of the passion,
And forming squads of tenderness.'

'You are,' they said, 'you are a man unjust one
In the clear daylight of falsehood days.
You are the culprit in all cases,
Whatever the case may be.'

Scaffolds stood erect on the land
To hang my words, for my decorated letters,
For my great number of pens.
They put in the heart of a pit
All my free letters,
My words and my great number of pens.
They collected firewood,
Poured oil on it,
And from a distance threw a lighted match,
Which turned my heart on fire,
And fires spread out
In all directions.

Index of First Lines

They said, 'Who are you?' 185
They said, 'Your poetry is not a good material 74

'Welcome, please feel at home! 121
We were away from our home country, 91
When I think of you 79

Yesterday and today for me are the same. 18
You, staying put in your burrow, 25
You, valley! 151
You, who have bewitched me and forsaken me: 169